W9-BPK-279

MORE THAN A MOVIE

20 FUN SPECIALS FOR YOUR CHILDREN'S MINISTRY

Group

Loveland, Colorado

www.group.com

Group resources actually work!

This Group resource helps you focus on **"The 1 Thing™"**— a life-changing relationship with Jesus Christ. "The 1 Thing" incorporates our **R.E.A.L.** approach to ministry. It reinforces a growing friendship with Jesus, encourages long-term learning, and results in life transformation, because it's:

Relational
Learner-to-learner interaction enhances learning and builds Christian friendships.

Experiential
What learners experience through discussion and action sticks with them up to 9 times longer than what they simply hear or read.

Applicable
The aim of Christian education is to equip learners to be both hearers and doers of God's Word.

Learner-based
Learners understand and retain more when the learning process takes into consideration how they learn best.

More Than a Movie: 20 Fun Specials for Your Children's Ministry

Copyright © 2005 Group Publishing, Inc.

All rights reserved. No part of this book may be reproduced in any manner whatsoever without prior written permission from the publisher, except where noted in the text and in the case of brief quotations embodied in critical articles and reviews. For information, write Permissions, Group Publishing, Inc., Dept. PD, P.O. Box 481, Loveland, CO 80539.

Visit our Web site: **www.group.com**

Credits
Contributing Authors: Teryl Cartwright, John R. Cutshall, Ruthie Daniels, Scott M. Kinner, Trish Kline, Julie Lavender, Kristin Leard, Julie Meiklejohn, Jennifer Nystrom, Christina Schofield
Editor: Mikal Keefer
Chief Creative Officer: Joani Schultz
Copy Editor: Jessica Broderick
Art Director: Kari K. Monson
Print Production Artist: Tracy K. Hindman
Cover Art Director/Designer: Bambi Eitel
Illustrator: Jan Knudson
Production Manager: Peggy Naylor

Unless otherwise noted, Scripture taken from the HOLY BIBLE, NEW INTERNATIONAL VERSION®. Copyright © 1973, 1978, 1984 by International Bible Society. Used by permission of Zondervan Publishing House. All rights reserved.

Library of Congress Cataloging-in-Publication Data
More than a movie : 20 fun specials for your children's ministry / [contributing authors, Teryl Cartwright ... et al. ; editor, Mikal Keefer].
      p. cm.
    Includes indexes.
    ISBN 0-7644-2838-1 (pbk. : alk, paper)
  1. Church work with children. 2. Motion pictures--Religious aspects--Christianity. 3. Motion pictures--Moral and ethical aspects. 4. Motion pictures. I. Cartwright, Teryl. II. Keefer, Mikal, 1954-
    BV639.C4M75 2005
    268'.432--dc22
                                       2004026673

10 9 8 7 6 5 4 3 2 1   14 13 12 11 10 09 08 07 06 05
Printed in the United States of America.

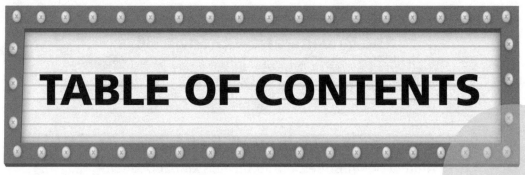

TABLE OF CONTENTS

INTRODUCTION

How to use More Than a Movie *in your children's ministry!*

Your kids *love* movies and videos—and now you'll harness the power and impact of full-length Hollywood favorites for Christian education.

"Wait a minute," you might be thinking. "*Hollywood?* In *Christian education?*" Absolutely…and it starts right here!

In this book, you'll find 20 fun-filled programs built around favorite family-friendly films—classic kids' movies you'll use to explore and debrief Bible truths. Each film is easy to find at your local video-rental store (we've checked!), and these are movies kids enjoy seeing again and again.

No matter how long the movie, we've carefully provided enough programming to fill two hours. For each of the 20 movies, you get…

• **Opening credits**—a wacky opening you'll lead as you set the stage for the movie and for Bible learning.

• **An intermission**—a pause packed with games and fun so children have the chance to stretch, grab snacks, and take bathroom breaks.

• **Closing credits**—a time for you to help kids debrief what they've experienced and how it connects to Bible learning.

• **A soundtrack special effect**—a fun audio track included on the CD that comes with this book.

Plus, you get **everything you need to make a *More Than a Movie* night complete**—decorating ideas, snack suggestions, and costuming tips!

More Than a Movie programs are perfect for multi-generational events, for retreats and evening programs, and to fill an evening for kids while their parents are in small groups.

Welcome to *More Than a Movie*—your ticket to fun Bible learning!

KEEPING IT LEGAL

You can legally show movies at your church—
and here's how!

You stop by the video store and pull a DVD off the shelf to show at church. As you drive home, a thought pulls at the corner of your attention. Are you actually allowed to screen a film in your children's ministry?

Are you breaking the law...or at least bending it? After all, it's not like you're charging *admission* or anything.

And what if the DVD *isn't* rented? What if you already own it? Then can you sit a dozen kids in front of a monitor at church and show them the movie without feeling guilty?

Here's the good news: There's a way for you to legally show almost any movie at church. There's even an *easy* way.

We'll get to the "easy" part in a moment. First, let's look at the legalities...

The Letter of the Law

"The Congress shall have Power...To promote the Progress of Science and useful Arts, by securing for limited Times to Authors and Inventors the exclusive Right to their respective Writings and Discoveries."
—U.S. Constitution, article 1, section 8

Those simple words from the Constitution have launched enough laws and lawsuits to keep courts busy for decades...and to inspire regulations that impact your children's ministry.

According to the U.S. Copyright Office (www.copyright.gov), a copyrighted work (including the videos recommended in this book) cannot be displayed publicly—*even if you bought the videos you're showing.*

You see, the license you received when you purchased *Gilligan Goes to Town* covers *home* use, not a public screening. If you want to watch the video with your family or friends in your living room, fine. It's completely legal as long as you don't charge for tickets and pocket the profits.

But when you show the same movie at church, that home license doesn't do the trick. And no matter how popular you are, a crowd of 200 kids and their parents gathered at church doesn't constitute a group of your closest friends.

If you want to screen a video at church, you'll need permission to do so from the copyright holder. Period.

The only exception to the rule that *might* allow you to show a video without a license is a tightly defined piece of section 110 of the copyright law that lets full-time, nonprofit academic institutions use some films in the context of face-to-face teaching activities.

But your Sunday school doesn't qualify.

Your pastor showing a movie clip as part of a sermon doesn't qualify.

And you showing an entire movie to your kids at church most *certainly* doesn't qualify.

So what can you do to be ethical, stay legal, and avoid paying fines that start at $500 and swiftly go up?

Get permission to show the movie…or buy a license.

Getting Permission

If *you'd* just spent $20 million creating a movie, you'd want to protect the showing of it too. You'd want to be paid when people saw your work or at least be asked before someone showed it for free.

The copyright law in America helps protect the right of filmmakers to profit from their work. And don't think you're off the hook if you happen to be reading this book in Canada or another country—your government undoubtedly has copyright laws too.

If you want to screen a movie in your church, you have two options: You can either get permission or buy a license.

You can contact the movie studios directly and request permission to show *Tarzan* to your elementary children, but be aware of two depressing realities:

• **The studio may say no.** Studios aren't obligated to agree to your request no matter how noble your intentions. You don't expect a grocery store to always donate food for your classroom snacks, do you? Or the local craft store to let you use its materials for free? Then don't expect movie studios to give you the OK to give away their property (a viewing experience) just because you asked. It's not necessarily that the studios are greedy or evil. They're in business, and they want to make a profit.

• **The studio may take months to answer.** It's sad but true: A request to show one movie one time in one church isn't going to be a top priority for a busy movie studio's legal department. It's not uncommon to wait months for a reply or not receive a reply at all.

So asking permission doesn't always work. What *else* can you do?

You can buy a license.

In fact, you may already have a license.

Buying a License

Christian Video Licensing International is an organization that acts as a clearinghouse between busy churches and busy movie studios. Rather than contact each studio individually with requests, you can pay an annual fee to CVLI and have a blanket permission to use many studios' films in the context of your church meetings.

There *are* limitations. You can't charge admission or hold your church meeting at a local theater where you invite strangers to watch the show after buying popcorn from you.

But for the purposes of this book, a CVLI license will do the trick for any movie from a studio that's agreed to be represented by the company…and most studios have.

If your church already shows video clips, check to see if a license has already been purchased. If so, you're covered. A license isn't just for one ministry in a congregation; it covers every ministry area.

Getting a license is easy. Visit www.cvli.org or call (888) 771-2854 to learn the details and get the ball rolling. Churches pay annual fees depending on the size of the congregation, so if you're a small church, you won't be expected to pay as much as a larger congregation.

There's really no excuse for using films illegally in our ministry settings. We can ask permission. We can buy licenses. We can take small steps to do what's required to execute our ministries with integrity.

FILLING EVERY SEAT IN THE HOUSE

Invite every child in your church—
and the entire neighborhood—
with photocopiable publicity help!

When you want kids to show up, it pays to advertise!

Whether you host a movie night for parents and kids or show a movie at a special kids-only program, you want a full house to enjoy the show.

And the photocopiable flier on page 13 will help!

Simply fill in the information, then make as many copies as you'd like for children in your church…and kids in the neighborhood.

When you're advertising a *More Than a Movie* event, start with the children in your ministry. Hand out fliers in church, Sunday school, midweek—anywhere kids attend your programs. And since children don't drive themselves to church, advertise to kids' parents, too.

More Than a Movie events are an easy way to introduce visitors to your ministry. If you want to pull in kids from the neighborhood, post fliers on community bulletin boards and in neighborhood stores.

But if you do invite children as a way of introducing them to your children's ministry, plan ahead for follow-up. How will you gather contact information? How will you reconnect with the children?

Get ready for your *More Than a Movie* programs. You're going to have a blast…and so will your kids!

More Than a Movie

ADMIT ONE   FREE

(or two or three…bring some friends!)

Now Showing:

Date:

Time:

Location:

Come enjoy a great movie, delicious snacks, and fun games. It's FREE! Questions? Call…

ADMIT ONE   FREE

(or two or three…bring some friends!)

More Than a Movie

Permission to photocopy this flier from *More Than a Movie* granted for local church use.
Copyright © Group Publishing, Inc., P.O. Box 481, Loveland, CO 80539. www.group.com

3

AND NOW FOR OUR FEATURE PRESENTATION:

The Movies!

20 films...20 complete two-hour programs...ready to go!

In the Spotlight:

101 DALMATIONS

G | **GENERAL AUDIENCES**
All Ages Admitted

1996, Walt Disney Pictures
Running time:
103 minutes

The Point: God gives us courage.

When a woman kidnaps puppies to create a fur coat, animals courageously cooperate to rescue the puppy prisoners. Your children will consider how they can be courageous too!

The Passage: Joshua 1:6-9

"Be strong and courageous, because you will lead these people to inherit the land I swore to their forefathers to give them. Be strong and very courageous. Be careful to obey all the law my servant Moses gave you; do not turn from it to the right or to the left, that you may be successful wherever you go. Do not let this Book of the Law depart from your mouth; meditate on it day and night, so that you may be careful to do everything written in it. Then you will be prosperous and successful. Have I not commanded you? Be strong and courageous. Do not be terrified; do not be discouraged, for the Lord your God will be with you wherever you go."

Notes to the Director

101 Dalmatians has a running time of 103 minutes, so you'll have just 17 minutes to help children make the connection between the animals' courage in the movie, the Israelites' courage, and the courage your children can receive by trusting God.

Environment

To get everyone in the mood to see this movie about Dalmatians, decorate the entire room in black spots! Cut out various sizes of spots from black construction paper, and attach the spots to the walls, chairs, tables, and so on. If you're using name tags, put black spots on them, too.

Play the "Barking Puppies" track of the *More Than a Movie* CD (track 19) as children arrive. Set your CD player on "repeat" so the track plays nonstop until the Opening Credits.

Before the movie, fill disposable bowls with dog biscuits to be used during the intermission as part of the Dog Bone Relay. Each bowl will need about 20 dog biscuits.

Carry the theme through to the snacks by serving graham cracker sticks, which resemble dog biscuits.

Cautions

This movie contains several scenes that might frighten very young children. Cruella De Vil can be sinister and has a very evil laugh, and she wants the puppies so she can make a coat out of them. The character Skinner is scary-looking, and his home is creepy. Horace and Jasper lock Nanny in the closet, and later they catch on fire.

Please note that Cruella smokes and calls people demeaning names such as "stupid," "idiot," and "imbecile."

Supplies

- CD player
- *More Than a Movie* CD
- transparent tape
- graham cracker sticks
- disposable bowls for crackers and dog biscuits
- chewable dog biscuits

Opening Credits (3 minutes)

Appear in a hat that features black polka-dot ears. Create this simple costume by cutting long, floppy ears from white fabric and taping or stapling them inside a cap. Glue on polka dots cut from black construction paper, and your costume is complete!

Gradually turn down the "Barking Puppies" track.

Say: **Welcome to our *More Than a Movie* night! We're screening *101 Dalmatians*, a film with an evil lady, a sinister plot, and a group of very courageous animals.**

Turn to someone sitting next to you, and decide which animal you think is the most courageous animal of all. You've got 20 seconds.

Have a few children share which animal they chose and why.

Say: **What I like about this movie is that it reminds me of how incredible things can happen when we're courageous. The animals in our movie will need to be very courageous, just as a man in the Bible named Joshua had to be courageous. You see, both the animals and Joshua were up against incredible odds. Let's watch the movie and see what happens. I'll tell you more about Joshua after the show.**

Do you all have your snacks? These snacks kind of remind me of dog biscuits! We'll have an intermission in about an hour, and that will be the time to load up on more dog biscuit snacks and take a bathroom break.

One more thing: During this movie, you'll hear Cruella De Vil laugh. When she laughs, I want you to yell, "Boo, hiss" back at her. Let's try it. I'll laugh, and you yell, "Boo, hiss."

Give your most sinister, evil laugh, then lead children and adults in shouting "Boo, hiss." Close the Opening Credits by saying: **Now let's watch the puppies.**

Dim the lights as the movie begins.

Be prepared to start the intermission about 50 minutes into the film, when Perdita crawls into the puppies' bed and Pongo lies down beside her.

Intermission (9 minutes)

After you have paused the movie, gradually turn the lights back on, and return to the front of the room.

Say: **Wow! What's going to happen to the puppies? In 10 minutes we'll resume, so this is a great time to take a bathroom break or get another bowl of graham cracker sticks. Puppies love to play with sticks; you can pretend to be a puppy while enjoying your graham cracker sticks.**

Join me in standing up, please. We're going to play a game while we take our intermission.

We're going to play Dog Bone Relay. If you came with your family, form a line with them from shortest to tallest. If you didn't come with your family, that's OK too. Just join another family; they'd love to have you! If you're part of a small family, join with another small family so you have at least four people on your team. No families here? Then join with other kids to form groups of four!

Please have the tallest person on your team come to the front and get one bowl filled with dog biscuits and one empty bowl. When you take them back to your team, place the full bowl on the floor at the beginning of the line and the empty bowl behind the last person in your line.

When I say "Go," I want the first person in your line to take one of the dog biscuits out of the bowl and pass it over his or her head to the person standing directly behind.

Each person in line will do this until the dog biscuit has been placed in the empty bowl at the end of the line. When the first dog biscuit is in the bowl, the person at the front of the line can get another one and start passing again. See how many dog biscuits your team can get into the bowl in 30 seconds. Ready? Go!

After 30 seconds, say "Stop," and allow the teams to count how many dog biscuits they were able to pass down their lines. Have teams each move the biscuits back to the first bowl and try again, seeing if they can break their first-round total.

You can continue to play the game, changing the way teams pass the dog biscuits down the lines by having them pass under their legs, behind their backs, with their eyes closed, and so on.

When nine minutes have passed, collect the dog biscuits, ask moviegoers to settle in, dim the lights, and pick up the movie where you paused it.

Closing Credits (5 minutes)

Say: **Quick! While you're still thinking about the movie, turn to a parent or partner, and discuss this question:**

• **What was the most courageous thing the animals had to do during the movie?**

You've got one minute to talk.

After a minute has passed, ask for several volunteers to share how they answered the question. Affirm their answers, then say: **I think it's cool that no matter how scary things got, the animals didn't lose their courage. Even when evil Cruella, mean Horace and Jasper, and wicked Skinner were after them, the animals kept on going.**

In the Bible there's a story about a man named Joshua. He became the leader

of God's people after Moses died.

Joshua knew how important it was to be strong and courageous. He encouraged his people to trust God and be courageous too.

One time, God told Joshua that he would help Joshua defeat his enemy if Joshua would be courageous and do exactly what God said to do. God told Joshua to have the Israelites march around the walls of Jericho one time a day for six days and then, on the seventh day, to march around the walls seven times and blow trumpets.

The Israelites could have been afraid to do what God wanted them to do. But they weren't afraid; they had courage. On the seventh day, when they marched around the walls and blew their trumpets, the walls came down.

God wants us to be courageous too. When we're afraid, we can ask God for courage. When things seem too hard, as they sometimes seemed for the puppies and for Joshua, we can remember what it says in Joshua 1:9: "Be strong and courageous. Do not be terrified; do not be discouraged, for the Lord your God will be with you wherever you go."

That's our movie tonight—thanks and good night!

Turn on the "Barking Puppies" track from the CD (track 19) to provide a background as the people leave.

Additional Themes Illustrated by This Movie:

loyalty and perseverance

In the Spotlight:

BABE

G | **GENERAL AUDIENCES**
All Ages Admitted

1995, Universal Pictures
Running time: 89 minutes

The Point: You're special—God created you that way.

Raised by sheepdogs, Babe (a pig) discovers that he's special. As your children experience this charming tale, they'll discover that, in Christ, *they're* special too!

The Passage: Psalm 139:14

"I praise you because I am fearfully and wonderfully made; your works are wonderful, I know that full well."

Notes to the Director

Babe has a running time of 89 minutes, so you'll have 31 minutes to help children make the connection between how Babe was special and how God has made each of us special!

Environment

Most of this movie takes place on a farm, so create a "barnyard" theme. Use red construction paper to cover the entry doors to your meeting room and strips of brown construction paper at an angle to look like wood slats on the doors. You can use more construction paper to cut out plants to hang on the walls if you'd like. And be sure to play the "Barnyard Sounds" track from the *More Than a Movie* CD (track 1) as children arrive. Set your CD player on "repeat" so the track plays nonstop until you're ready to start talking.

Carry the theme through to the snacks by serving animal crackers.

Cautions

This movie contains several scenes that might frighten very young children. There is some violence involving the sheepdogs, and a sheep is killed. Some scenes appear very dark as the animals fear for their lives.

Supplies

- CD player
- *More Than a Movie* CD
- animal crackers
- disposable bowls for crackers
- whistle for game during intermission (optional)

Opening Credits (7 minutes)

Cue the "Barnyard Sounds" track from the *More Than a Movie* CD (track 1), and play the rooster crowing at the beginning to get everyone's attention. Then turn the CD player off.

Walk in front of the screen wearing a straw hat and overalls or other stereotypical farm attire.

Say: **Welcome to our *More Than a Movie* night! We're screening *Babe*, a film about a special pig who was raised by sheepdogs.**

Turn to those close to you, and take turns answering this question:

• How do you think you would act if you had been raised by sheepdogs?

Take about one minute to share your response with those around you.

Encourage everyone to share and even act out answers until 60 seconds have passed.

Say: **I really like how this movie shows that differences are OK and that everyone is special.**

Let's each find a partner! Answer these questions as you talk with your partner. How would you be different if you

• lived 100 years ago?

• lived at the North Pole?

• were 20 years older than you are right now?

Give partners up to one minute to answer each question, then say: **People are different for lots of reasons—their age, where they live, even when they live. And people are special for lots of reasons too. We'll talk more about being special after the movie is over.**

Do you all have your snacks? We'll have an intermission in about an hour, and that will be the time to load up on more snacks and take a bathroom break.

One more thing: During this movie you'll see mice appear on the screen, and you'll hear them talk or sing as the scenes in the movie change. Whenever you see these mice, I want you to silently act scared by lifting your feet up and covering your mouth, as if you're surprised to see mice in the room. Let's try it a couple of times. Pretend you see mice on the screen right now!

Encourage the children and adults to lift their feet and cover their mouths as if they are surprised and afraid.

Dim the lights as the movie begins.

Be prepared to start the intermission about 59 minutes into the film, when the farmer takes the shotgun shells out of his gun.

Intermission (16 minutes)

After you have paused the movie, gradually turn the lights back on, and return to the front of the room.

Say: **What a relief! Babe seems to be safe, so now we'll take a short break. In 16 minutes we'll resume, so this is a great time to take a bathroom break or get another bowl of animal crackers. Just remember, be back and ready for the mice and the next scene when 16 minutes are up.**

Stand up, please. We're going to play a game while we take our intermission.

This game will get participants moving and making some noise!

Say: **This game is called Animal Mix-Up. You'll need to listen closely as I call out a number and the name of an animal. You'll get into small groups after you hear the number and the animal.**

The number will let you know how many to have in your group. If I say "three cows," you'll need to get into groups of three. Once you have exactly that number in your group, you'll get down on your hands and knees and act like cows.

The name of the animal will let you know what sounds and actions to make to act out that animal in your group. So if I say "three cows," what will you do after you have three people and are on your hands and knees?

Encourage everyone to moo and move around like a cow.

Say: **In each round, there may be some special people who don't have enough to make a full group. These special people will meet here by me to either find enough for a group or act out the animal with me.**

Let's do a practice round to be sure we are all ready to play. Ready? Let's get in groups of three chickens!

Encourage older children and adults to help the younger ones as they all get in groups of three and begin to act like chickens.

If you have a whistle, blow it at the end of each round to help get everyone's attention. Things will become rowdy!

Say: **OK, everyone, get back up. Walk around and mix with different people. Let's see how fast we can get in our groups and start making some noise! Get in groups of four ducks!**

Continue to encourage the participants during each round, and allow time for groups to form. Between each round, say: **Good job. Now everyone stand and mix up!**

Use the suggestions below or create some of your own.

- **Get in groups of three horses!**
- **Get in groups of two pigs!**
- **Get in groups of three dogs!**
- **Get in groups of four sheep!**
- **Get in groups of two giraffes!**

Allow for confused looks and unknown sounds, then proceed with the game as before.

- **Get in groups of one cat!**
- **Get in groups of three mice!**
- **Good job!**

If there's time, you can play the "Barnyard Sounds" track from the *More Than a Movie* CD (track 1) and allow participants to act out the animals they hear.

When 16 minutes have passed, ask moviegoers to settle in, dim the lights, and pick up the movie where you paused it.

Closing Credits (8 minutes)

Say: **Let's take a couple of minutes to discuss the movie. Get in groups of three or four farmers, and take a minute to discuss these questions:**

- **What are some ways Babe seemed special to you?**
- **What are some ways Babe treated others as special?**

• **What are some ways other characters in the movie were special?**

Allow about 30 seconds of discussion between each question. Repeat questions out loud if necessary.

After a couple of minutes, bring everyone back together, and ask for some volunteers to share their responses to the questions.

Say: **In this movie, we can see that every character in this movie was special. That's true of each person as well. God has created us to be unique and special, and God loves each of us very much!**

Psalm 139:14 says, "I praise you because I am fearfully and wonderfully made; your works are wonderful, I know that full well."

Each one of you here is special! You have special abilities and characteristics all your own. But more importantly, *you will always be loved by God,* and God will always think you are special! He created you that way!

That's our movie tonight—thanks and good night!

Additional Themes Illustrated by This Movie:

encouragement, kindness, and purpose

In the Spotlight:

BEAUTY AND THE BEAST

G | **GENERAL AUDIENCES**
All Ages Admitted

1991, Walt Disney Pictures
Running time: 84 minutes

The Point: Love has the power to transform us.

Bitter and trapped in a beast's body, a prince experiences the transforming power of love...just as your children can experience the transforming power of God's love!

The Passage: 1 John 4:7-8

"Dear friends, let us love one another, for love comes from God. Everyone who loves has been born of God and knows God. Whoever does not love does not know God, because God is love."

Notes to the Director

Beauty and the Beast is 84 minutes long. You will use the remaining 36 minutes to help children see how love transformed the beast and discover that God's love can have the same transforming power in their own lives.

Environment

Create a castle-like environment for the children to enter. Using butcher paper painted blue, construct a moat inside the entrance to the room where you'll screen the movie.

Using brown butcher paper, create a bridge over the moat so children can walk across it as they enter the room. Keep the room lighting dim, and play the "Thunder and Lightning" track on the *More Than a Movie* CD (track 2) as the children enter. Set your CD player on "repeat" so the track plays continuously until the movie begins.

Set aside an area of the room for making mirrors. As children arrive, send them to a table in that area to make a mirror. Tell children that everyone will need a mirror for a special game they will play during the movie.

It will help to have a volunteer at the mirror-making station to assist children in their efforts. Ask your volunteer to create several extra mirrors to give to kids who arrive after the movie has started.

To make a mirror, staple or tape a small dessert-size paper plate to a craft stick. Cover the paper plate with tin foil, and voilà! A mirror!

In the movie, the young teacup's name is "Chip." In keeping with the theme of the movie, serve various kinds of chips as a snack. Children can eat the chips off additional paper plates.

Before children arrive, cut out at least one paper heart from red construction paper for each participant. You'll use these hearts for a game during the intermission.

Cautions

This movie contains several scenes where wolves chase people in dark and rainy weather. The first—and most intense—chase scene is toward the beginning of the movie.

After the intermission, when Belle leaves the castle for the first time, she is chased by wolves through the forest, and this scene could possibly scare children.

Another scene that might scare children is when the Beast appears for the first time. This is also toward the beginning of the movie.

Supplies

- CD player
- *More Than a Movie* CD
- dessert-size paper plates
- craft sticks
- tape
- tin foil
- various kinds of chips
- red construction paper
- scissors
- Hershey's Kisses or Hugs candies

Opening Credits (10 minutes)

When children arrive, have them make their "mirrors" before sitting down. Remind children to hold on to their mirrors because they will need them throughout the movie.

Enter the room carrying a hoe or pitchfork, and pretend to be a confused villager. Acting confused and nervous, ask the children if they've seen the Beast.

Say: **Have you seen him? Have you seen that mean, scary Beast? I don't know what to do. We've got to find him fast, and that won't be easy in this terrible storm!**

Quick, hold up the mirrors you made. Those mirrors let you see things that happen in other places. Does anyone see the Beast in a mirror? I guess he's not here, so we'll just have to watch the movie to see what happened to him. Set down the hoe or pitchfork you're carrying.

Before we begin the movie, turn to the person sitting next to you, and tell him or her about a time you were *really* afraid of something or someone. Tell your partner how you got over that fear or if you're still afraid today. Share a quick example from your own life.

As children talk, gradually turn down the soundtrack until it's silent.

After children share with their partners, ask for volunteers to tell the large group the things that sometimes make them afraid.

Pick up your pitchfork or hoe again.

Say: **We're about to watch a movie about a prince who was turned into a beast because he wasn't loving or kind to someone. The prince was only willing to be kind to people who looked a certain way.**

Unfortunately for the prince, the person he didn't treat well had magical powers, and she turned the prince into a beast.

To become a prince again, the Beast has to learn to share his love with another person. Let's find out if he's able to do it!

During the movie, you'll see that the Beast has a magic mirror like the one you made! Every time you see the Beast or someone else using the magic mirror, hold up your mirror and say, "God is love!"

Let's practice two times. Ready? Hold up your mirrors and say, "God is love!" Let's do it one more time.

Allow children to practice again. Then say: **Good job. Let's start the movie!**

Be prepared to start the intermission about 42 minutes into the film. This will be after the dishes sing to Belle and she says, "Perhaps you'd like to take me. I'm sure you know everything there is to know about the castle."

Intermission (16 minutes)

Pause the movie, turn on the lights, and walk to the front of the room with your hoe or pitchfork.

Say: **Wow! Things are getting exciting for Belle and the Beast! We're going to take a short break. This is a great time to go to the bathroom or grab some chips to eat during the rest of the movie.**

Before we get back to the movie, let's play a game called Musical Hearts.

Move children to a part of the room where there's space to play Musical Hearts. Depending on the number of children in attendance, you might want to split into two or more groups. This game is a lot like Musical Chairs, but instead of chairs, the children will stand on the red construction-paper hearts you've already cut out.

Lay the hearts on the floor in a circle or in the shape of a very large heart. Have each child stand on one.

Begin playing the "Heart to Heart" track from the *More Than a Movie* CD (track 3), and have children walk from heart to heart. As children walk, remove one heart from those on the floor. When you stop the music, all of the children should be standing on a heart except for one child.

Tell that child that he or she is still in the game. But to keep playing, he or she has to run around the circle (or heart) and give everyone a quick high-five. Then he or she can put the heart back on the floor.

Play this game several times.

As children are heading back to their seats, give them each a Hershey's Kiss or Hug candy and remind them that God is love!

Encourage children to get more chips if they want and then sit down so they can watch the rest of the movie.

Closing Credits (10 minutes)

Say: **What a great movie! Hold up your mirrors and say, "God is love"** again. Lead children in saying the phrase.

In the movie, the Beast is transformed by love. His heart is changed forever. What are some things the Beast did during the movie to show us he was changing for the better? Share your answers with the person sitting beside you.

Allow time for children to share their insights, then ask for volunteers to share what they discovered in their discussions.

Say: **God loves us so much that his love has the power to change our hearts. When we let God's love into our hearts, what are some things that might change? Share some of your ideas with the person sitting next to you.**

Allow time for children to share their insights, then ask for volunteers to share what they discovered about how God's love can change our hearts and how we live every day.

Say: **God's love is so powerful that it can permanently change us. When we ask God to live in our hearts, we're telling him that we want to be his friend forever. We want to live a life that is pleasing to God now, and we want to live with him in heaven forever.**

Before we go home, let's hold up our mirrors one more time and say together, "God is love!" And remember that God's love transforms us!

Additional Themes Illustrated by This Movie:

courage, friendship, loneliness, and transformation

In the Spotlight:

A BUG'S LIFE

G GENERAL AUDIENCES
All Ages Admitted

1998, Pixar Animation Studios and Walt Disney Pictures
Running time: 96 minutes

The Point: Little people can make a big difference.

An ant's plan to hire warrior bugs to protect his friends and family from bullies backfires...but he discovers even little ants can make a difference. Your kids will discover they can make a difference too!

The Passage: 1 Timothy 4:12

"Don't let anyone look down on you because you are young, but set an example for the believers in speech, in life, in love, in faith and in purity."

Notes to the Director

A Bug's Life has a running time of 96 minutes, so you'll have 24 minutes to help children make the connection between the difference the bugs made in this movie and how God can use even the youngest people to make a big difference!

Environment

This movie takes place down low on the ground, so create a "grassy" theme. Hang green crepe paper in a hallway or doorway so children brush through it as they enter the room where you'll screen the movie. And be sure to have the "Bugs" track of the *More Than a Movie* CD (track 4) playing when children arrive. Set the CD player on "repeat" so the track plays nonstop until the movie begins.

Carry the theme through to the snacks by serving pretzel "sticks" throughout the movie and sugar cookies with green icing during the intermission.

Cautions

This movie contains some scenes that might frighten very young children. Large bugs bully the ants and smaller bugs in a few scenes, and a bird later attacks and catches the larger bug. The attack is not graphic, but it is obvious that the bug becomes lunch.

Supplies

- CD player
- *More Than a Movie* CD
- pretzel sticks
- sugar cookies with green icing (one per participant)
- napkins or disposable plates for snacks

Opening Credits (5 minutes)

Walk in front of the screen wearing a hat or headband with antennas and, if possible, a green shirt and green pants.

Say: **Welcome to our *More Than a Movie* night! We're screening *A Bug's Life*, a film about ants that get bullied by grasshoppers. We'll find out what happens when one brave ant hires warrior bugs to protect his friends and family from the bullies.**

Turn to someone sitting next to you, and tell him or her what kind of bug you'd want to be if you had to choose one. You've got 10 seconds.

Now turn to someone different, and tell him or her what kind of bug sometimes scares you. You've got 10 seconds.

Let's get in groups of four or five and discuss this question:

• What are some things that bugs are good at doing? Try to come up with at least three things.

Allow groups to discuss their answers for about one minute and then have them return to their seats.

Say: **I like this movie because it shows that even if you're small, you can do some very important things.**

After the movie, we'll talk about things we can do to serve God and help others.

Do you all have snacks? We'll have an intermission in about an hour, and that will be the time to load up on more snacks and take a bathroom break.

One more thing: During the movie, you'll see some of the bugs flying. Whenever you see a bug flying, I want you to put your hands on your shoulders and flap your "wings" along with the bugs. Let's practice.

Lead children and adults in flapping their arms, then close the Opening Credits by saying: **Now let's watch *A Bug's Life*!**

Dim the lights and turn off the CD player as the movie begins.

Be prepared to start the intermission 56 minutes into the film, when the grasshoppers start flying after the line "Let's ride."

Intermission (12 minutes)

After you have paused the movie, gradually turn the lights back on, and return to the front of the room.

Say: **What an adventure! In 12 minutes we'll resume, so this is a great time to take a bathroom break or get some more pretzel sticks.**

Join me in standing up, please. We're going to play a game during Intermission.

For this game, you'll need to divide your group into four teams that are roughly the same size. Have each team go to a corner (or area) of the room. Then have teams proceed as described below.

Say: **For this game, your team needs to secretly choose a bug that you'll imitate for the other teams. As each team acts out and makes the noises of its chosen bug, the other three teams will try to guess what bug is being imitated.**

I'll give you two minutes to discuss and choose a bug. Remember, you want to come up with actions and sounds that everyone in your group can do and that will allow the other teams to guess your bug. You may also want to have two

bugs in mind in case another group uses your first choice—but it is OK to use the same bug several times.

After two minutes, bring the groups closer together, and allow each group to present its bug imitation. Plan on about 30 seconds to a minute for each group, with a little bit of time between each performance for applause and for bringing the next group front and center. Encourage groups to give extra clues if they stump the guessing teams.

Then say: **Good job, everyone! As a reward for your efforts, you all get an ant hill covered in grass!**

Distribute a sugar cookie with green icing to every moviegoer as a treat.

If there's time, play the "Bugs" track on the CD again (track 4). Have the kids act out as many bugs as they can hear.

After 12 minutes, ask moviegoers to settle in. Remind them to flap their arms when they see bugs flying. Dim the lights, and pick up the movie where you paused it.

Closing Credits (7 minutes)

Say: **Get with one or two other people, and discuss these questions:**

• **Who was your favorite character in the movie? I'll give you 30 seconds to share your answers.**

• **What do you think was the most exciting thing that happened in the movie? I'll give you one minute so everyone in your group can share an answer.**

• **What are some big things you remember these little bugs doing to defend themselves? Take another minute to discuss these things in your group.**

When the time is up, have moviegoers return to their seats. Ask for volunteers to share their responses to the last question with the whole group. Offer positive feedback for each response, and after several responses, ask:

• **What are some excuses the smaller bugs could have given so they wouldn't have to stand up to the larger bugs?**

Allow some discussion. Point out that excuses *were* given earlier in the movie, but eventually the little bugs overcame those negative attitudes and gave their best to stand up for their friends and families.

Say: **1 Timothy 4:12 says, "Don't let anyone look down on you because you are young, but set an example for the believers in speech, in life, in love, in faith and in purity."**

This verse shows us that being young is not an excuse. It also doesn't matter how other people view us. Rather than worry about things we *can't* do, we can focus on the many things we *can* do.

One thing each of us can do is set an example. We can set an example by how we talk, how we act, how we treat others, how we trust God, and how we do good things. By doing the things God wants us to do, we can help others see who God is and how much he loves each of us.

We can be like Flik and do good things even when other people aren't ready to good things. It's brave to do the right thing when others aren't willing or before anyone else will do it. The "right thing" can be as small and simple as picking up a candy wrapper on the ground or as big as sharing your faith. You can set

an example that's good for others to see—and follow.

Actually, doing good and helping others is always a big deal! And it can make a big difference to people around you, even if you aren't very big or very old!

That's our movie tonight—thanks and good night!

Additional Themes Illustrated by This Movie:

David and Goliath, fear, friendship, gifts, and significance

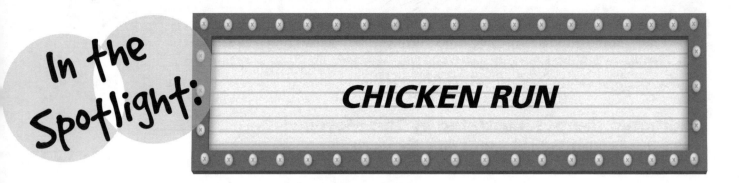

In the Spotlight:

CHICKEN RUN

G | **GENERAL AUDIENCES**
All Ages Admitted

2000, DreamWorks SKG
Running time: 84 minutes

The Point: Freedom in Christ is a gift.

As these clay-animated chickens fight against all odds to find freedom, you'll help children understand the importance of *true* freedom—in Christ!

The Passage: Galatians 5:1a

"It is for freedom that Christ has set us free."

Notes to the Director

Chicken Run has a running time of 84 minutes. With the remaining 36 minutes, you'll help the children understand that freedom in Christ is a gift.

Environment

Since this movie takes place in a barn, create a barn-like atmosphere for the children. Use butcher paper you've painted red to cover the door to the room where you'll screen the movie. Then place stuffed farm animals around the room. As kids enter, play the "Chicken Sounds" track of the *More Than a Movie* CD (track 5). Set your CD player on "repeat" so the track plays nonstop until the movie begins.

Enter wearing a chicken-in-a-box costume.

Create the costume using a large cardboard box for the body of the chicken. Cut out the bottom flaps to create openings for your feet. Cut out rectangular wing flaps on the sides of the box, leaving the top of the wings attached to the box so the wings rise as you lift your arms. Make sure the wings are long enough to cover your arms. And consider looping a piece of twine around each cardboard wing to keep your arms against the wings—that way it's easy for the wings to move when your arms move.

At the top of the box, cut out a rectangle. The hole should be big enough for your head to fit through but small enough so the box doesn't slip off your shoulders.

Cut "feathers" out of yellow construction paper, and tape them to the box. Now you look just like a chicken!

Serve Cocoa Pebbles, puffed wheat cereal, or another round cereal to children in paper bowls for a snack. Describe the snack as "chicken feed." Encourage kids to try eating the snack by pecking—the way chickens eat!

Cautions

There's a scene showing two chickens in a pie-making machine that might frighten young children. The chickens emerge intact, but it's an intense scene.

Supplies

- CD player
- *More Than a Movie* CD
- paper bowls
- Cocoa Pebbles or other cereal
- rubber chicken wrapped in a gift box

Opening Credits (12 minutes)

Enter the room wearing your chicken-in-a-box costume.

Say: **Hello! I'm Chicken-in-a-Box, and at this *More Than a Movie* night, we'll watch a film in which a lot of chickens do their best to *not* look like me!**

We're going to watch *Chicken Run*. This movie is about a bunch of chickens who are trying to escape the chicken farm where they all live. On the chicken farm, they are forced to lay eggs and do things they don't like to do.

Before we start, I want to share something I brought with me: a present! Hold up a wrapped gift box that has a rubber chicken inside, then give the box to a child you've selected at random. **I want you to have this gift. But before you open it, please answer a few questions:**

- **Is today Christmas?** (The child will answer "no.")
- **Is today your birthday?** (The child will answer "no"—hopefully!)
- **Then why do you think you deserve this gift?**

Allow the child to answer, then continue: **Here's my point. You don't have to do anything to deserve this gift because it's a gift freely given. To receive it, you only have to unwrap it. Go ahead and open the gift, and hold up what you received.**

When the child holds up the rubber chicken, say: **Wow! A rubber chicken! Just like me—and just for you! What a great gift. Did you have to pay me for the gift? Did you have to work hard for the gift? Did you have to do anything for the gift? No!**

Now turn to someone sitting next to you, and answer these questions:
- **What's the best gift you've ever received?**
- **What's the best gift you've ever given to another person?**
- **What gift would you most like to give someone?**

After pairs talk, ask for some volunteers to share their answers with the larger group.

Say: **Our movie tonight is about some chickens who are trying to be free. They have to work really hard for their freedom, but here's a secret: You don't. You can have freedom from your sins, and all you have to do is unwrap the present God wants to give you. We'll talk more about that after the movie.**

One more thing: As we watch the movie, look for scenes where chickens are learning to fly and running down a runway. When you see that happen, yell, "Chickens can't fly!"

Let's practice one time. I'll be the chicken trying to fly. Run across the room flapping your arms. **Ready? One, two, three: "Chickens can't fly!" Great job! Let's watch the movie.**

Be prepared to start the intermission 45 minutes into the film. This will be after the chickens have their dance.

Intermission (14 minutes)

After you've paused the movie, turn the lights back on, and walk like a chicken to the front of the room—still wearing your chicken-in-a-box costume, of course!

Say: **Wow! Those chickens had to work really hard to get in shape so they could learn to fly. Let's do a few chicken aerobics ourselves! As we're doing our aerobics, feel free to get a refill of chicken feed or take a bathroom break.**

Everybody up on your feet!

First, stretch your chicken wings (arms) **up to the sky. Touch the sky, and then bend over and touch your claws.**

Now wiggle your wings, and flap them as if you're getting ready to lift off. As you flap your wings, run in place.

Wow, you look like a lot of chickens who are ready to fly! Now keep flapping your wings while you bend at your knees and stick out your backside. You look like a bunch of chickens ready to waddle! Let's waddle around the room—follow me and do what I do!

Lead children around the room, waddling and moving your wings. Squat down low, run fast or slow, or waddle in place as you play this version of Follow the Leader.

After a minute or so, say: **OK, let's waddle back to our chairs and have a seat. Thanks for participating in chicken aerobics with me!**

In the movie, the chickens are really struggling when it comes to flying. Turn to the person sitting next to you and answer these questions:

• **What's something difficult you have to do?**

• **How could you get better at doing that difficult task?**

For instance, maybe you're learning to play the tuba. It's tough! But if you practiced more or got help from a tuba player, it would be easier.

After children have had a chance to talk, draw attention back to yourself.

Say: **Now that we've all stretched and taken a break, let's watch the end of the movie.**

Closing Credits (10 minutes)

Say: **Wasn't that a great movie? Raise your hand if you think the chickens will be happy in paradise forever. I think so! Ask:**

• **How did the chickens finally figure out how to get free?** Allow for some answers.

Say: **One thing is for sure: They had to work really hard to end up in paradise. And they certainly had some scary moments along the way!**

The good news for us is that we don't have to work as hard as the chickens did for our freedom. It's a gift from God!

Remember the gift our friend unwrapped before the movie? All [name of child who unwrapped gift] **had to do to have the gift was unwrap it and accept it.** [Name of child] **didn't earn it. In fact, when the gift is something so expensive and wonderful as a rubber chicken, it** *can't* **be earned. I wouldn't have sold it for $100!**

God really does offer us a precious gift that we can't begin to pay for. He offers us his love and, through Christ Jesus, his forgiveness.

Those are priceless gifts, but if you're willing to receive them, they're yours. If you'd like to learn more about receiving God's love and forgiveness, come talk to me after the movie. I'll tell you all about it!

Thank you for coming to the chicken farm and watching our movie. Good night!

Additional Themes Illustrated by This Movie:

perseverance, teamwork, and trust

In the Spotlight:

THE EMPEROR'S NEW GROOVE

G | **GENERAL AUDIENCES**
All Ages Admitted

2000, Walt Disney Pictures
Running time: 78 minutes

The Point: Be humble.

An arrogant emperor is turned into a llama and discovers the need for humility. This movie will help your kids discover that they need humility too.

The Passage: Psalm 25:9

"He guides the humble in what is right and teaches them his way."

Notes to the Director

The Emperor's New Groove has a running time of 78 minutes, so you'll have 42 minutes to help children understand that humility is a characteristic God wants to see in those who serve him.

Environment

The emperor wants a new summer home with a view—and doesn't mind tearing down a family's house to accomplish his goal. So hang signs that have the words "Condemned" and "New Site of Summer Palace" around the screening area. Some construction cones, shovels, and sledgehammers will complete the effect.

Be sure to play the "Parade March" track of the *More Than a Movie* CD (track 6) as children arrive. Set your CD player on "repeat" so the track plays nonstop until you start the program.

Serve sandwich-style cookies, such as Oreos, for the snack. This snack will illustrate a teaching point during the Closing Credits.

Cautions

The emperor is often rude and insulting, showing a lack of empathy and respect to others. Urge children to *not* emulate him!

Supplies

- CD player
- *More Than a Movie* CD
- sandwich-style cookies, such as Oreos
- napkins
- blank index cards

Opening Credits (7 minutes)

Before you make an appearance, start the "Royal Entrance" track on the *More Than a Movie* CD (track 7). Walk in wearing a crown like the one worn by the emperor in this film. A crown of paper will suffice.

Stop in front of the screen, and look around regally until the music ends. The track is about 30 seconds long.

Say: **Welcome to our *More Than a Movie* night! Notice anything different about me?** Tilt your head and pose so children will know you're showing off.

Yep, I'm wearing a crown—just like the one the emperor wears in our movie. The movie is called *The Emperor's New Groove*. An emperor is like a king, so you can call me King [fill in your name] **or Emperor** [fill in your name]. **Either is fine by me.**

Now I'm going to tell you my first command. Turn to a partner and answer this question:

• Kings wear crowns like mine. What *other* things are true about kings?

After moviegoers talk for a minute, ask for volunteers to share their answers. Affirm their answers, and have a good time trying to include the insights into your kingly (or queenly!) demeanor.

Say: **Great insights! You know, we can read about several kings in the Bible, including King David.**

King David didn't start out as a king. When he was a boy, he was a shepherd who cared for sheep. He had to chase around after them and keep them safe from wolves and other animals that like to have sheep for lunch.

When David became a king, he remembered what it was like to have a hard job, such as being a shepherd. He remembered what it was like to be a soldier, too.

And he *always* remembered what it was like to be loved by God and to love God back.

All of that kept David humble. He knew he had faults, and he knew what it was like to live out under the stars instead of in a palace.

In our movie, we'll see another king—an emperor—and he's nothing like King David! See for yourself as we watch *The Emperor's New Groove*!

Do you all have your snacks? Let's wait one minute so everyone can load up on snacks. We'll have an intermission in about 30 minutes.

One more thing: During this movie, our emperor becomes an animal. When this happens, let's all yell, "Get a shave, dude!"

Lead children and adults in shouting, "Get a shave, dude!" three times, then close the Opening Credits by saying: **Let's start the movie!**

Dim the lights.

Be prepared to start the intermission about 30 minutes into the film, when the emperor (as a llama) walks into the foreboding woods and Pacha says, "Takes care of my problem."

> Who can name me a King in the Bible

Intermission (20 minutes)

Once you have paused the movie, gradually turn the lights back on, and return to the front of the room.

Say: **What an adventure! The movie will begin again in about 20 minutes. This is a great time to take a bathroom break or grab a few more cookies.**

Join me in standing up, please. We're going to play a couple of games while we take our intermission.

This activity teaches a principle while getting everyone up and energized!

Say: **The first game is Follow the Leader! You know how to play that game, right? Everyone lines up behind the leader and does all the things the leader does. Since I'm wearing this very special emperor's crown, I'll be the leader. So line up and follow me.**

Keep the activities to simple movements, such as hopping, skipping, jumping, or standing on one leg. Also use your hands and arms—put one arm in the air, both arms in the air, your hands on top of your head, and so on.

When you have finished, say: **When you play Follow the Leader, you have to do what your leader does. So it's really important who we follow.**

Turn to a partner and discuss this question:

• **Whose example is it good to follow?**

Give children 30 seconds to brainstorm, then ask volunteers to share their ideas. Affirm answers as much as possible. Ask:

• **Have any of you noticed how mean and rude the emperor in our movie is? What are some words the emperor never, ever uses? He never uses words like** *please* **and** *excuse me*. **What other words do polite, courteous people use that our emperor doesn't seem to know?** Listen for words such as *thank you, you're welcome,* and *you go first*.

Do you know why the emperor never says "please," "thank you," or "excuse me"? It's because he doesn't care about anybody but himself.

The emperor is full of pride—and pride causes you to think only about how great you are! And when you think you're great and think only about yourself, you don't care about the feelings or needs of anyone else.

Jesus told us that we should be humble and think about others. Boy, that sure doesn't sound like the emperor, does it? When we think about other people, we act polite, and our actions show that we care about their feelings.

Pass out a stack of eight cards to each moviegoer.

Say: **We're going to play a game that the emperor wouldn't be good at. But you'll be great! It's called Please Take a Card.**

Here's how you play. The goal is to give away all your cards by approaching other people and saying, "Please take a card." When you say that, the person has to take one of your cards as a gift.

And that person can't just turn around and ask you to take a card from him or her. There can only be one card exchanged in each conversation.

You'll have three minutes to get rid of your cards. Ready? Go!

After three minutes, say: **OK, that's it! Who managed to get rid of all their cards? Great job! Who still has cards? How about if you win too by giving them all to me?**

Collect the cards and then say: **Time to watch the rest of the movie! If you'd like, get another cookie and then return to your seat.**

Resume the movie.

Closing Credits (15 minutes)

After the movie ends, say: **Turn to a partner and tell that person what you think about the emperor now.**

After children have had a few minutes to talk, ask for volunteers to share their assessments of the emperor.

Say: **Do you remember Pacha saying that it's the *inside* that counts? Well, our snacks were sort of like that.**

I noticed that some of you ate your cookies by pulling them apart and eating the icing first. What was on the inside was most important to you.

In our lives, what's on the inside matters a lot too. On the inside, we can be prideful and rude, or we can be humble and thoughtful of others.

The emperor changed from proud to humble, but it wasn't an easy change. He had to be turned into a llama first! Hopefully God won't have to let that happen to us before we will be humble.

Let's do one more activity together before we wrap up. Please get up and stand over here. Indicate a clear area of the room.

Everyone find a partner. I want the person who is wearing the most blue to be the emperor. The other person in each pair will be the servant.

Emperors, I'm going to give you 30 seconds to each think of an assignment for your servant. The assignment has to be something that will help out a person at our movie night. For instance, if my shoes were untied, the servant could tie them for me.

Or maybe the servant could give me a quick back rub or a friendly pat on the back. I'd like that. It would help me feel good.

When I give you the signal, the emperors will send their servants out to help others. The job has to be accomplished in just 30 seconds, and it has to be something your servant is willing to do.

Ready to think of something for your servants to do, emperors? Start thinking.

When 30 seconds have passed, say: **Emperors, tell your servants what to do. And now, servants, get busy! Go!**

After 30 seconds, ask partners to get back together.

Say: **Way to go! You're all changing jobs. Servants, you're now appointed kings. Emperors, you're now the servants.**

Kings, think of something your servants can do to help someone here in the room. Got an idea? Tell your servants, and they'll have 30 seconds to do the job.

Ready? Go!

After 30 seconds, ask pairs to sit down together and discuss the following:

• **Which position did you enjoy most: being in charge or being the servant?**

• **What's hard about being a servant?**

• **Do you like being told what to do? Why or why not?**

Ask for volunteers to share what they discovered in their discussions. Affirm answers, then sum up.

Say: **To be a good servant, you've got to be humble. You've got to care about others and put their needs first. You've got to be willing to serve!**

Take off your crown, and put it aside.

Say: **Psalm 25:9 says, "He guides the humble in what is right and teaches them his way." I want to be humble so I can be a good servant of God.**

The emperor in the movie learned that being humble and serving his people was a good thing. When we're humble, we can serve people—and we can also serve God! So be humble!

That's our movie for tonight. Good night!

Additional Themes Illustrated by This Movie:

courtesy, honesty, and respect

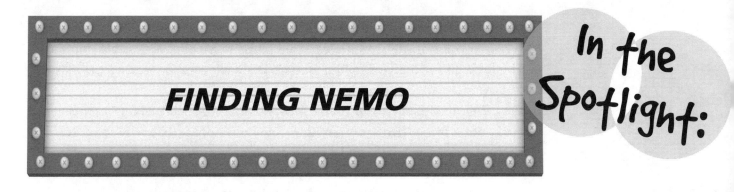

FINDING NEMO

The Point: God seeks us.

A timid clownfish sets out to save his kidnapped son—no matter what. Use this movie to help children consider how much God has done to save us from our sins.

The Passage: Romans 5:6-7

"You see, at just the right time, when we were still powerless, Christ died for the ungodly. Very rarely will anyone die for a righteous man, though for a good man someone might possibly dare to die. But God demonstrates his own love for us in this: While we were still sinners, Christ died for us."

Notes to the Director

Finding Nemo has a running time of 100 minutes, so you'll have just 20 minutes to help children make the connection between Marlin's love for his son, Nemo, and God's love for his children—us!

Environment

Most of this movie takes place underwater, so create an "underwater" theme. Hang blue crepe paper in a hallway or doorway so children brush through it as they enter the room where you'll screen the movie. And be sure to play the "Underwater" track of the *More Than a Movie* CD (track 8) as children arrive. Set your CD player on "repeat" so the track plays nonstop until the movie begins.

Carry the theme through to the snacks by serving Goldfish crackers and gummy worms.

Cautions

This movie contains several scenes that might frighten very young children. A large shark chases Marlin and Dory through a submarine, and Nemo later takes a perilous journey through an aquarium filtration system. Both scenes are brief, and no one is hurt in either scene.

Supplies

- CD player
- *More Than a Movie* CD
- Goldfish crackers
- gummy worms (one per participant)
- disposable bowls for crackers

G | GENERAL AUDIENCES
All Ages Admitted

2003, Pixar Animation Studios and Walt Disney Pictures
Running time: 100 minutes

CAUTION

Opening Credits (5 minutes)

Walk in front of the screen wearing a scuba mask and, if possible, flippers. It will be difficult for the kids to hear you clearly while you're wearing the mask, so take it off after a few moments.

Say: **Welcome to our *More Than a Movie* night! We're screening *Finding Nemo*, a film about a father fish's journey to recover his kidnapped son. Along the way, we'll meet sharks, jellyfish, and a dentist—three very scary kinds of creatures!**

Turn to someone sitting next to you and decide if you would rather face a shark, a jellyfish, or a dentist and why. You've got 20 seconds.

Ask for a show of hands to find out how many people were most willing to face a shark, a jellyfish, or a dentist. If the dentist scores well—relatively speaking—point out that kids should remember this the next time they get a cavity filled.

Say: **What I like about this movie is that it reminds me of *another* father who did everything he could to be reunited with his children.**

Before we screen the movie, let me tell you about this other dad. His kids weren't kidnapped by divers, as little Nemo was. Instead, they stuck out their chests and said, "We don't need you, Dad. We don't have to obey your rules. We'll get through life on our own!"

The father could have just said, "Fine, then. You're on your own. Who needs you?" That's what the kids deserved.

Instead, the father reminded his children about the rules. He made the rules really clear so they'd know exactly what they had to do to stay in a relationship with the father.

But the children ignored the rules.

Then the father sent messengers to explain what the children needed to do to heal their relationship with their dad. The messengers knew exactly what the dad wanted to say.

The children ignored the messengers. Sometimes, the kids *hurt* the messengers!

So the dad decided to do something even better—but I'll tell you about that after the movie.

Do you all have your snacks? We'll have an intermission in about an hour, and that will be the time to load up on more snacks and take a bathroom break.

One more thing: During this movie, you'll hear the line "Fish are friends, not food." Every time you hear that line, I want you to yell back, "That's right, Bruce!" Let's try it three times.

Lead children and adults in shouting, "That's right, Bruce!" three times. Then close the Opening Credits by saying: **Now let's go find Nemo!**

Dim the lights and turn off the CD player as the movie begins.

Be prepared to start the intermission at about 57 minutes into the film, when birds are flying and you hear the line, "There's one dedicated father."

Intermission (10 minutes)

Once you have paused the movie, gradually turn the lights back on, and return to the front of the room.

Say: **What an adventure! In 10 minutes we'll resume, so this is a great time to take a bathroom break or get another bowl of Goldfish crackers. Just remember, though, that fish are friends, not food!**

Join me in standing up, please. We're going to play a couple games while we take our intermission.

The first game is designed to get participants who've been seated for a long time stretching and moving…but don't tell them that!

Say: **The first game is One Fin, Two Fin. Remember that Nemo has one fin that's less developed than the other. In spite of what some other fish saw as a handicap, he could do anything they could do. Let's see how well we can use one or both of our fins. Do what I call out. Ready?**

- **Reach as high as you can with just one fin. Now reach as high as you can with both fins.**
- **Touch your toes with one fin. Now with both fins.**
- **Close your eyes, and touch your nose with your left fin. Now with your right fin.**
- **Open one eye, and stretch both fins out in front of you. See if you can touch your index fingers on the first try.**
- **Now open both eyes, and try to touch your index fingers together behind your back on the first try. Now behind your head. Now behind someone *else's* head!**
- **Do five jumping jacks while waving your fins. Now while keeping your fins at your sides.**

Good job, you finny friends!

Marlin needed help searching for Nemo. I need your help looking for a list of things too.

Find a new partner. Your team's job is to bring me what I'm looking for. If your team is the first to bring me what I'm looking for, you'll win Nemo's favorite treat: a gummy worm! Yum! You can win more than once.

- **I'm looking for a picture of Abraham Lincoln.** (This is on a U.S. $1 bill or penny.)
- **I'm looking for someone who can translate a sentence into another language.** (Ask for a translation of "Fish are friends, not food.")
- **I'm looking for a library card.**
- **I'm looking for a receipt.**
- **I'm looking for a coin that was minted in 1992.**
- **I'm looking for someone blowing a bubble.**
- **I'm looking for someone who'd like to have a gummy worm.**

Distribute a gummy worm to every moviegoer as a treat.

If there's time, ask for volunteers to tell you their funniest jokes. See if any kid qualifies as "Honorary Clownfish"!

When 10 minutes have passed, ask moviegoers to settle in, dim the lights, and pick up the movie where you paused it.

Closing Credits (5 minutes)

Say: **While you're still thinking about the movie, quickly turn to a parent or partner and discuss this question:**

• **What's the coolest thing Marlin did while searching for Nemo? You've got one minute to talk.**

While moviegoers are talking, turn the "Underwater" track of the CD (track 8) back on. After a minute has passed, ask for several volunteers to share how they answered the question. Affirm their answers, then say: **I think it's cool that no matter what, this dad didn't give up. He kept doing whatever he could to keep searching for Nemo. Marlin loved his son, and he wanted his son to be with him!**

The dad I was telling you about earlier—the one whose children walked away and disobeyed him—explained the rules to them and then sent messengers, and he absolutely didn't give up.

That dad was God the Father. When people chose to sin instead of obeying him, God didn't just give up on people. He gave us the Ten Commandments so we'd know how to live. But we didn't obey the Ten Commandments—none of us have. Raise your hand if you've never, ever told a lie. See? God sent prophets to tell us what to do. We usually didn't listen.

Then God did the most amazing thing: He sent his Son, Jesus, to rescue us from our sins by dying in our place!

God loves you that much. He thinks you're that important. God is seeking a friendship with you so you can be with him forever in heaven. That's good news!

Marlin loved Nemo and kept looking for Nemo. God loves you and is looking for you. Nemo didn't know how to find his way home, but I can tell you how to find your way to heaven. It's through Jesus.

If you don't know about Jesus, I'll be glad to talk to you about him tonight. Just hang around, and let's talk.

That's our movie tonight—thanks and good night!

Additional Themes Illustrated by This Movie:

courage, loyalty, and perseverance

THE GREAT MUPPET CAPER

In the Spotlight:

The Point: We can help others.

While Kermit, Fozzie, and Gonzo visit England and try to help avert a jewel theft, your kids will discover that helping others is a great thing.

The Passage: Ecclesiastes 4:10

"If one falls down, his friend can help him up. But pity the man who falls and has no one to help him up!"

Notes to the Director

The Great Muppet Caper has a running time of 95 minutes, so you'll have 25 minutes to help children connect how the Muppets helped each other and how we can help each other.

Environment

Most of this movie takes place in the city of London, so create an "English city" theme. Set out large cardboard boxes with rectangle windows drawn on them to represent tall buildings. Label one box "Happiness Hotel." Use a box to make the Big Ben clock as well.

And be sure to play the "Cityscapes" track of the *More Than a Movie* CD (track 9) as children arrive. Set your CD player on "repeat" so the track plays nonstop until the movie begins.

Reinforce the Muppet characters theme by serving gummy bears, gummy frogs, and Teddy Grahams.

Cautions

This movie contains several stunts and falls that don't injure the Muppets but will injure children who try the same stunts at home. In your best British accent, remind children that they shouldn't be daft enough to try the same tricks themselves or they'll end up in the surgery (doctor's office) receiving plaster (adhesive bandages).

There's also questionable language in the song "Happiness Hotel," but the instance is so brief that it may go unnoticed by the children.

G | GENERAL AUDIENCES
All Ages Admitted

1981, Universal Pictures
Running time: 95 minutes

CAUTION

Supplies

- CD player
- *More Than a Movie* CD
- Bible
- Teddy Grahams
- gummy frogs and bears
- disposable bowls for snacks
- pens
- plastic wrap taped into "baseballs" or soft foam balls (one for every four participants)
- napkins

Opening Credits (5 minutes)

Run out in front of the screen wearing a suit, suspenders, a bicycle helmet, a backpack, and a sheet with ropes attached like a parachute. Fold the "parachute" as you talk.

Say: **Tallyho, chums. I've just jetted in from jolly ol' England to welcome you to our *More Than a Movie* night! We'll view *The Great Muppet Caper*, a hilarious film about some daring chaps who not only help catch a jewel thief but also help some new friends along the way. In this film, you'll see lorries, lifts, flats, and, of course, lots of posh people. That means trucks, elevators, apartments, and fancy folks. We use different words for things in London, something you'll discover in this film!**

Before we start, turn to someone sitting near you, and for 30 seconds discuss this question:

- **Do you think it's easier to help a friend or a stranger?**

Remember to give a reason for your answer. You have 30 seconds! Go!

Take a vote to see which answer was more prevalent, and ask for times and situations where the opposite answer might also be true.

Say: **What I like about this movie is that the Muppet characters help their friends *and* strangers. Jesus helped friends and strangers too.**

Before we screen the film, let me tell you about a time Jesus helped a paralyzed man. You can read about it in the book of Luke. Open a Bible to Luke 5:17-20.

This man's friends brought him to Jesus, but they couldn't get close enough to ask Jesus for help because there was a crowd around the house where Jesus was teaching. So the friends cut a hole in the roof of the house and lowered their paralyzed friend down while everyone watched. Jesus helped the paralyzed man walk because the man's friends showed faith in him.

Jesus had another reason for helping the man too, but I'll tell you about that after the film.

Do you all have your snacks? During Intermission, which will be in about an hour, you can get more biscuits if you feel peckish or go to the loo if you need a bathroom break.

One more thing: During this movie, you'll see the Muppets fall or run into things. I want you to help our Muppet friends by calling, "Look out!" every time you see them about to get into trouble. Let's yell, "Look out!" three times to practice helping the Muppets.

Lead children and adults in shouting, "Look out!" three times. Then close the Opening Credits by saying: **Right-o, then. Let's see how the Muppets help both friends and strangers!**

Dim the lights and turn off the CD player as the movie begins.

Be prepared to start the intermission about 53 minutes into the film, when the door opens and Gonzo's photograph is ruined.

Intermission (15 minutes)

Once you have paused the movie, turn the lights back on, and return to the front of the room.

Play the "Camera Clicks" track of the *More Than a Movie* CD (track 10). Set your CD player on "repeat" so the track plays nonstop.

Say: **Please stand up now. We're going to play a few games while we take our intermission. If you want to visit the restroom or get a drink of water, feel free to do so anytime during the next 15 minutes.**

The first game gets everyone to stretch and move after sitting so long, but don't admit this!

Say: **The first game is called Freeze Frame. Remember how Gonzo was always taking pictures during the movie? I want you to get with two or three other people and freeze for a picture when I yell, "Say cheese!" The catch is that when I say that, you have to be stretched into an action shot showing how one of you is helping the others.**

For example, you could pose as if you were helping someone cross the street or helping to get a ball out of a tree. When I yell "Action!" quickly scramble into another pose before the camera goes off again. Ready? Play the "Camera Clicks" track on the CD for about three minutes, then ask the groups to discuss the following:

• **How did you feel knowing that a camera was going to catch you doing a good deed?**

• **Why do you think some people help each other when they know someone is watching?**

• **How do you feel knowing that God sees everything you do?**

Say: **Our second game is a lot like a scene you'll see near the end of the movie. Get together in groups of four, then toss a ball to each other like a game of Hot Potato.**

During the first few minutes of play, I want you to say, "I'm going to help _____" when you throw the ball. Fill in the name of the person to whom you're throwing the ball. Your group can go faster and faster, but throw carefully and see how long you can keep the ball from touching the ground.

After two minutes, stop the game, and encourage two foursomes to join so there are eight people in a circle. Have groups keep both balls going simultaneously and stop calling out names. The goal is to move fast but still keep the balls in the air.

After a minute, stop the game, and ask people to form pairs. Remind them that the movie will be starting soon and it's a good time to visit the restroom or get a drink of water and more snacks. Then ask pairs the following question:

• **How far would you go to help someone?**

Say: **The Muppets went all the way to London! This time, as you quickly pass the ball back and forth with your partner, I want you to name places where you can help people. You can name towns, countries, or even buildings such as hospitals and churches. The object is to keep naming a different place each time you throw until your group can't think of any other places. Go!**

Play for a minute or two longer and then stop the game.

Say: **It was hard to keep going, wasn't it? Sometimes it's hard to keep helping out, too. Being persistent is important when you try to help others.**

If there's time, ask for volunteers to do Muppet voice impressions.

When 15 minutes have passed, ask moviegoers to settle in, dim the lights, and pick up the movie where you paused it. Say: **Let's see what the Muppets do next.**

Closing Credits (5 minutes)

Say: **While you're still thinking about the movie, quickly turn to a parent or partner and discuss these questions:**
• **Why did the Muppets help others?**
• **Why do *we* help others?**
Say: **You've got 90 seconds to talk.**

After the time has passed, ask for several volunteers to share how they answered the questions. Affirm their answers, then say: **The Muppets had lots of reasons to help others. The Bible tells us that *we* should help others so we can show God's love.**

There are many ways to help others. In a moment, you'll get a napkin and pen so you can write down one way to help someone. If you need help spelling, ask a grown-up for help.

Distribute materials. After 45 seconds, say: **Let's stand, open up our napkins, and pitch them toward the ceiling like a parachute. Then catch someone else's napkin so you can read a new way to help someone this week. Ready? Go!**

After napkins have been caught, read aloud Ecclesiastes 4:10.

Say: **Everyone needs help, and we can show God's love by helping others. This week, help someone in the way described on your napkin. We can help others— and that shows others God's love!**

That's our film, mates! Good night!

Additional Themes Illustrated by This Movie:

love, loyalty, and perseverance

HOMEWARD BOUND: THE INCREDIBLE JOURNEY

The Point: True friendship is a gift.

Three pets set out on a journey to find their family. They discover that they need each other and that friendship is a gift. Your kids will discover the same things!

The Passage: John 15:12-13

"My command is this: Love each other as I have loved you. Greater love has no one than this, that he lay down his life for his friends."

Notes to the Director

Homeward Bound: The Incredible Journey has a running time of 84 minutes, so you'll have 36 minutes to talk about the special gift of friendship.

Environment

Most of this movie takes place in the great outdoors, so create a mountainside theme. Throw a beige or green blanket over a table and chairs to create some rolling hills. Find plants or small trees used for decoration, or set up artificial Christmas trees. A small pile of wood can resemble a campfire. Placing snacks in a dog food bowl will help children feel like pets!

Cautions

This movie contains several scenes that might frighten very young children. A mountain lion chases Chance and Shadow, and Sassy is carried away over river rapids. A porcupine buries some spines in Chance's nose.

Supplies

- CD player
- *More Than a Movie* CD
- bite-size candy (Hershey's Hugs and Kisses, mini Snickers, and mini 3 Musketeers bars)
- dog food bowl
- handkerchief loaded with fragrance (such as vanilla or vinegar)
- Bible

G GENERAL AUDIENCES
All Ages Admitted

1993, Walt Disney Pictures
Running time: 84 minutes

CAUTION

Opening Credits (10 minutes)

Before children arrive, hide a fragrant handkerchief (soaked ahead of time in vinegar or vanilla) somewhere in the room. The scent should be noticeable when near the handkerchief but not overwhelming. As children arrive, engage the "bloodhounds" right away in a hunt for the hankie. Once it's been found, introduce tonight's movie wearing your spiffy dogcatcher uniform.

Say: **Welcome to our *More Than a Movie* night! We're screening *Homeward Bound: The Incredible Journey*, a film about the friendship three pets have with their family and with each other.**

Invite children to turn to partners and talk about their own pets for a minute.

Then say: **The pets in this movie are named Chance, Shadow, and Sassy. Turn to a new partner, and see if you can pick a silly name for a pet turtle. What's the silliest name you can think of?**

After 30 seconds, ask volunteers to share the names they chose.

Say: **In this movie, Chance, Shadow, and Sassy take off on a big adventure to find their family. Along the way, they learn about the importance of friendship and find it in some unexpected places. Not only are they devoted to their masters, but they are also devoted to each other—even though dogs and cats don't always see eye to eye.**

There are lots of stories in the Bible about friendships. But the one I like most is about the king who left his beautiful home to search for lost friends. He was treated terribly. Still, he saw his mission through because he loved his friends, he was loyal to them, and he knew he could rescue them.

The special king I'm talking about is Jesus. His friendship means more than anything in life.

Friendship is a special gift—a gift of love, a gift of loyalty, and even a gift of laughs. We'll talk more about these gifts a little later, but right now, let's watch the movie. We'll have an intermission in about an hour to eat a snack and take a bathroom break.

Close the Opening Credits by leading everyone in their best dog howl! Challenge them to howl again when they hear this line in the movie: "Dogs rule; cats drool."

Dim the lights as the movie begins.

Be prepared to start the intermission about 49 minutes into the film, when Sassy hears two dogs in the distance and says, "What's that?"

Intermission (20 minutes)

Once you've paused the movie, gradually turn the lights back on, and return to the front of the room.

Say: **Will Chance, Shadow, and Sassy ever find their way back home? You'll have to wait to find out because it's time for Intermission! If you'd like, use the restroom or get a drink of water while the rest of us play Dog Tag!**

This game will get those stiff legs and bottoms moving!

First, designate one person to be the dogcatcher and one person to be the doggies' best friend. Kids will play on their hands and knees in an open space until they're tagged by the dogcatcher. When someone gets tagged, that child must "play dead" until the doggies' best friend comes to his or her aid and scratches

Perfume can sometimes trigger allergies, so it's best to avoid using it to create your fragrant handkerchief.

the child behind the ear. During the game, you can designate additional children to be the doggies' best friends.

Explain the game, and then "let the dogs out!" Play for several minutes before passing around a dog food dish full of Hershey's Hugs and Kisses and mini Snickers and 3 Musketeers bars. Let each child pick out one candy bar (or two or three Hugs and Kisses). If you have diabetics or dieters in the group, plan a special snack for them.

Point out that the candy has connections with true friendship: the gifts of love (Hugs and Kisses), loyalty (3 Musketeers), and laughs (Snickers).

Say: **Did that silly game teach you anything about friendship? An important part of friendship is helping out our friends, just as Shadow, Chance, and Sassy helped one another. Some of you took a risk to help your friends even though you might have been tagged yourself.**

Open your Bible, and read John 15:12-13 aloud.

Say: **Real friendship means loving someone so much that you do what's good for that friend without considering what you want for yourself. And loyalty means that you don't forget about the friend when loving that person gets hard.**

Another gift that comes with friendship is laughter. I'll bet each of you could tell a story about a time a friend cheered you up when you felt down. In the last part of this movie, you'll see how Chance encourages his friend when Shadow feels that he just can't go on. Let's play a quick game about laughter.

Start the "Laugh Track" segment on the *More Than a Movie* CD (track 11). Put it on continuous play throughout this game.

Explain that half of the kids will try to keep a straight face while the other kids try to make their friends laugh or crack a smile by making faces, funny sounds, and so on. Be sure the children know they *aren't* allowed to touch or tickle any players to evoke laughter. After a while, have children switch places and play again.

At the end of the intermission, ask moviegoers to settle in. Dim the lights, and pick up the movie where you paused it.

Closing Credits (6 minutes)

When the movie is over, help the children think about the special friendship these animals had and make the connection that friendship is a special gift.

Say: **Chance, Shadow, and Sassy went to a lot of trouble to find their family. Turn to a partner and discuss this question:**

• What scary things did the three animals face because they loved their friends?

Ask for volunteers to suggest answers to the question.

Then say: **The animals were determined to find their family at any cost because they wanted to be with them. Their strong friendship helped them through even the scariest moments.**

Jesus faced the scariest things imaginable to be your friend. He was willing to face death because of his great love and loyalty toward you, and even when you can't see him, he is there, cheering you on when you are down. Jesus is the very best friend you could ask for.

But friendship isn't meant to be one-sided. In the movie, each character loved and looked after the others. How will you respond to Jesus' gift of friendship? What kind of friend will you be to him? How can you show him your love, loyalty, and joy?

If you don't know about Jesus, I'm available at any time to introduce you to the greatest friend you could ever know. If you'd like, you can stick around tonight, and we'll talk.

Jesus is the perfect gift for all occasions!

Additional Themes Illustrated by This Movie:

hope, overcoming obstacles, and teamwork

THE HUNCHBACK OF NOTRE DAME

The Point: God looks at the heart.

A cathedral bell ringer faces ridicule because people see only his deformed body, not his heart. Your children will consider how God views people.

The Passage: 1 Samuel 16:7b

"The Lord does not look at the things man looks at. Man looks at the outward appearance, but the Lord looks at the heart."

Notes to the Director

The Hunchback of Notre Dame has a running time of 91 minutes, so you will have almost 30 minutes to help children learn not to judge by appearances. God looks at our insides, and we're called to do the same!

Environment

This movie is set in medieval France. Much of the action happens during a festival, so create a party theme!

Hang multicolored pieces of crepe paper and large paper bells (available at party stores) on the walls and ceiling around the screening room. To create bells instead, invert lightweight plastic flowerpots, and cover them with tinfoil. Hang balloons, too—in a child's world, balloons almost scream "party."

Play the "Bells" track of the *More Than a Movie* CD (track 12) as children arrive. Set your CD player on "repeat" so the track plays nonstop until the movie begins.

Carry the French party theme through to the snacks by serving seedless grapes and square cheese crackers. To avoid any choking hazards, slice the grapes in two for the benefit of young children.

Cautions

This movie contains several scenes that might frighten very young children, especially scenes throughout the movie that show the brutal treatment of Quasimodo. Also be aware that Judge Frollo sings a suggestive song.

Supplies

- CD player
- *More Than a Movie* CD
- grapes
- square cheese crackers

G | **GENERAL AUDIENCES**
All Ages Admitted

1996, Walt Disney Pictures
Running time: 91 minutes

53

- disposable bowls for crackers and grapes
- six-inch squares of paper (one per person)
- hand puppet
- pens and markers
- bell

Opening Credits (9 minutes)

Walk in wearing a jester cap and brightly colored striped clothing, suggesting a jester's costume. Wear a hand puppet, and allow it to speak as directed in a thick French accent.

Say: **Bonjour! We're very glad to see you. Welcome to our *More Than a Movie* night!**

Puppet: **Listen! I hear bells. Why do you think there are bells in here today?**

Say: **I don't know. Maybe the children have some ideas.** Allow children to suggest possible answers.

Bells are an important part of our movie, *The Hunchback of Notre Dame.* Notre Dame is a very famous church in France, and Quasimodo, our story's hero, lives in the bell tower there. But that's not the *only* reason we want to talk about bells today.

Puppet: **Oui, oui. *Belle* is also a French word. It means "beautiful."**

Say: **Turn to someone sitting next to you, and answer this question:**

- **What makes a bell beautiful? You've got 30 seconds.**

As children talk, put down the puppet, and give each participant a square sheet of paper. If you have lots of moviegoers, recruit some volunteer help for this task.

Ask for volunteers to share what they decided in their discussions. Affirm their answers, then pick up a real bell and ring it.

Say: **Listen to this sound. Bells are considered beautiful more for what they do than for how they look. We can't judge real beauty just by how something looks.**

There's a man in the Bible who once judged somebody by looks only. Samuel was looking for a king who'd rule over God's people, so he looked for a tall, strong man. But God looks at our hearts, and God knew that a little boy named David would make the best king—no matter how David looked on the outside.

Samuel was judging kings based on how they looked. God was judging based on their hearts. In our movie, people judge Quasimodo by how he looks. You'll see for yourself how well that goes.

But before we start the movie, let's turn our pieces of paper into bells we can ring when we hear the famous bells of Notre Dame.

Hold up a piece of paper, and demonstrate how to create a bell. See the illustrations on page 55 for guidance.

Say: **First, take the top *left* corner of your square, and fold it away from you. If you peek at the back of the paper, you'll see that you've now made a triangle that's hiding from you.**

Now take the top *right* corner of your square, and fold it away from you, folding it to the same size and shape as the first triangle you made. Hold the paper so that both corners are hidden from you.

How to Make a Jester Cap

Pin four brightly colored socks around the bottom of a knit winter hat. The pins should go through the top part of each sock, and the toes should point up toward the top of the hat. Fold the bottom of the cap halfway up to hide the bottom of the socks and make the socks hang down only slightly. Pin jingle bells to the end of each sock toe.

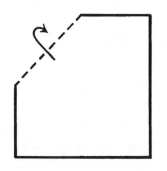 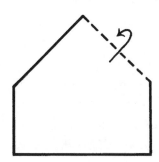 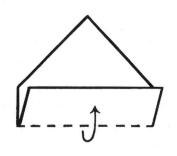

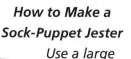

How to Make a Sock-Puppet Jester
Use a large mitten or a sock with a third of the toe folded inward to create a mouth. Fold the bottom of a glove halfway up, then securely pin the glove on top of the mitten or sock to make a jester cap. Pin jingle bells on the glove's fingertips. Add eyes to the puppet with a marker, or tape cotton balls with sticker dots for irises onto the puppet.

Finally, hold the bottom of your square, and fold the whole bottom edge up an inch facing you. This is the bottom rim of your bell.

Every time you hear a bell in the movie, I want you to hold up your bell and rock it back and forth as if *it* is ringing too. Let's try that, and since we're practicing, yell "ding dong" when you ring your bell.

Lead children and adults in waving their bells several times, then close the Opening Credits by pulling the puppet back on your hand and having the puppet say: **Now let's ring in our show!**

Dim the lights and turn off the CD player as the movie begins.

Be prepared to start the intermission about 46 minutes into the film, just as Esmeralda finishes her song in the sanctuary by singing, "God bless the outcasts, children of God."

Intermission (15 minutes)

Once you've paused the movie, gradually turn on the lights, and return to the front of the room.

Say: **What a powerful song! In 15 minutes we'll resume, so this is a great time to take a bathroom break or get a bowl of cheese crackers and grapes. It's French snack food!**

Turn on the CD to the "Bells" track again (track 12).

Say: **Let's play a few games during our intermission. I want you to find and stand by someone who has a different hair color from you. Try to only stand with one person, but, if necessary, you can have up to four people standing together. Ready? Go!**

• **Now find and stand by someone with a different eye color.**

• **Find someone with a different height from you.**

• **Find someone who is a different age from you.**

• **Now find someone who is a different gender (in other words, find a boy if you're a girl, and find a girl if you're a boy).**

• **Finally, find someone with a different address from you.**

Ask: • **Why do you think God made us all different?** Allow kids to suggest some answers, and affirm each one.

Say: **We have a lot of differences, don't we? I'm glad we can celebrate being unique. In our movie, we've already seen that there are many ways to be beautiful. The Bible tells us, "The Lord does not look at the things man looks at. Man looks at the outward appearance, but the Lord looks at the heart." God knows** that the best kind of beauty is the kind that's inside.

Instruct kids to get in two straight lines of about the same length. Have the lines form about a foot apart, and once children are in the two lines, have kids turn so they're facing away from each other.

Say: **In a few moments, I'm going to ask you to close your eyes so you can't see. Don't worry—nobody is going to touch you or spray water on you or anything. I want to move some of you around so you don't know who's standing around you. Ready to close your eyes? Do that now, and stay absolutely silent—no talking!**

Rearrange several children, then say: **Keep your eyes closed. I want you to guess who's directly behind you by listening to the person's voice as he or she repeats something after me.**

What's going to make this really hard is that you have to listen *while you're speaking*. In a moment, I'll ask you to say, "Ding dong, hear the gong." That's sort of a bell message. Ready? Repeat after me: "Ding dong, hear the gong."

If you think you know who's behind you, reach back and touch that person as you say his or her name.

Give kids time to guess who's behind them, then say:

If your name was guessed correctly, tell your partner that he or she was right without turning around. If your name wasn't guessed correctly, you will answer questions to help your partner discover your name.

To discover who's behind you, you can't turn around and look at the person or ask the person's name. But you *can* ask questions that require one-word answers. For instance, you can ask for the person's grade level or where the person goes to school. Maybe the person behind you is a friend, or maybe he or she is a stranger. Keep asking questions until you guess the person's name.

You may play this game more than once.

If there's still time, ask volunteers to share French phrases and words they know, especially any they've heard in the movie. For more fun, invite a person who's fluent in French to come and translate things the children want to hear translated.

When the 15 minutes are up, ask everyone to sit back down, dim the lights, and start the movie where you paused it.

Closing Credits (5 minutes)

Say: **While you're still thinking about the movie, turn to a parent or partner, and discuss these questions.**

- **How did the child at the end of the movie set an example for others?**
- **How can we set an example too? You've got one minute to talk.**

While moviegoers are talking, turn the "Bells" track back on (track 12). After a minute has passed, ask volunteers to share their answers. Then say: **We need to set an example about how to look for beauty on people's insides instead of just people's outsides. That's how God views us—and we can view other people the same way. God looks at the heart!**

Please hold up your bells again. Pause to let children find and hold up their bells. **When you hear bells, let them be a reminder to look at people's hearts.**

In a moment, I'm going to ask you to trade bells with your partner. When you do, write or draw something nice on your partner's bell that explains what's beautiful about that person's heart.

For instance, you could write, "You're a great friend!" or "You always see the good in others." When you give back your partner's bell, he or she will have a reminder of how God has made him or her beautiful on the inside.

Take a moment to get a pen or marker and write or draw something nice on your partner's bell. Hand out pens and markers.

Allow 30 seconds, then ask kids to return the bells to their owners.

Say: If you would like to hear more about how God looks at our hearts, I'll be glad to talk to you in a little bit. Just stick around, and we'll talk.

Put the puppet back on your hand, and let the puppet close the evening by saying, "That's our movie tonight—merci and au revoir!"

Additional Themes Illustrated by This Movie:

acceptance, courage, and vision

Unofficial French Pronunciation Guide

The accented syllables are in italics.
- bonjour (bon-*zhoor*): good day or hello
- bonsoir (bon-*swar*): good evening or good night
- oui (*wee*): yes
- belle (*bell*): beautiful
- merci (mehr-*see*): thank you
- au revoir (oh ruh-*vwahr*): goodbye

In the Spotlight:

ICE AGE

PG **PARENTAL GUIDANCE SUGGESTED**
SOME MATERIAL MAY NOT BE SUITABLE FOR CHILDREN
(for mild peril)

2002, Fox Animation
Studios
Running time: 81 minutes

The Point: We can forgive others.

As a woolly mammoth learns to forgive, your children will consider how they've been forgiven—and how they can forgive others.

The Passage: Ephesians 4:32

"Be kind and compassionate to one another, forgiving each other, just as in Christ God forgave you."

Notes to the Director

Ice Age has a running time of 81 minutes, so you'll have almost 40 minutes to teach your kids about forgiveness—God's forgiveness toward us and how we should forgive each other!

Environment

In this movie, we watch a group of mismatched ice age animals travel with a baby to find the baby's family. Your kids will help create your own icy tundra in the opening activity.

To enhance the room, you can drape white sheets over furniture to create the illusion of a snow-covered wilderness. Tape blue butcher paper on the walls; it will be used in all the activities.

Hide packing "peanuts" (foam pieces used for packing by shippers) all over the room for the intermission scavenger hunt. Be sure to play the "Howling Wind" track of the *More Than a Movie* CD (track 13) as the children arrive. Set your CD player on "repeat" so the track plays nonstop until the movie begins.

Carry the theme through to the snacks by serving animal crackers. Tell children that the crackers are mini dinosaurs!

Cautions

This movie contains some scenes that might frighten very young children. There is a saber-toothed tiger attack, and the main characters face some perilous predicaments.

CAUTION

Supplies

- CD player
- *More Than a Movie* CD
- white paper
- scissors
- crayons
- animal crackers
- disposable bowls for crackers
- foam packing "peanuts"

Opening Credits (10 minutes)

Walk in front of the screen wearing a winter parka and some mittens.

Say: **Welcome to our *More Than a Movie* night! We're screening *Ice Age*, a film about a group of misfit animals trying to get a human baby back to his family. We'll see a wooly mammoth, a saber-toothed tiger, and a sloth all trying to take care of a baby.**

It's the beginning of the ice age, so snow is beginning to fall. We're going to make our own snow for the room.

Pass out a piece of white paper and, if you have enough, a pair of scissors to each child. If you don't have enough scissors, instruct children to share.

Demonstrate how to fold the piece of paper three times and then cut out pieces along the folds, so that when the paper is unfolded, it looks like a beautiful snowflake. Have children tape their snowflakes onto the butcher-papered walls to resemble a snowstorm.

Then say: **Look at all of the snowflakes. Each one of them is different and unique. Some may look similar, but look carefully and you'll discover that no two are alike.**

It's like that with people: Each of us is unique and different.

Turn to a partner, and tell that person one thing that's unique and different about you that most people don't know. Maybe your middle name is Gertrude. Or maybe you were born in a foreign country or you've met someone famous. You've got 30 seconds to tell what's special about you, and then your partner will have 30 seconds. Go!

After kids have shared, say: **We're all different, but there's one way we're all the same—God loves us. And there's another way we're the same, too—God will forgive us if we ask him.**

Sometimes we find it hard to forgive others, especially people who hurt us or who are different from us. God will forgive us, but we don't always forgive each other.

We'll talk more about forgiveness during our intermission and after the movie.

Do you all have your snacks? We'll have an intermission in about an hour, and that will be the time to load up on more snacks and take a bathroom break.

One more thing: During this movie, you'll see a funny little squirrel struggling to get a nut. Every time you see him struggle with that nut, say, "Oh, no, not again!" Let's try that together.

Lead children and adults in shouting, "Oh, no, not again!" three times, then close the Opening Credits by saying: **Let's enter the *Ice Age*!**

Dim the lights and turn off the CD player as the movie begins.

Be prepared to start the intermission about 56 minutes into the film, after the animals get out of the cave with the hieroglyphics and Sid says, "I don't know about you guys, but we are the weirdest herd I've ever seen."

Intermission (15 minutes)

Once you have paused the movie, gradually turn the lights back on, and return to the front of the room.

Say: **What an adventure! In about 15 minutes we'll resume, so this is a great time to take a bathroom break or stock up on more snacks.**

Before we do our activity, we're going to have a little scavenger hunt.

The scavenger hunt is designed to get participants who've been seated a long time stretching and moving...but don't tell them that!

Say: **We're going to find some "nuts" to go with our animal crackers. I've hidden lots of packing peanuts all over the room. Take your bowls and gather as many nuts as you can, because it's going to be a *long* winter. You'll have three minutes. Ready? Go!**

Give the children three minutes to find peanuts, then instruct children to come back to their seats.

Say: **Now let's think about something we just saw in the movie. While Sid and Manny were in the cave, they saw some drawings on the walls. These are called hieroglyphics. Hieroglyphics are pictures used to tell stories. What story did we see on the wall of the cave?** Pause for and affirm the answers you hear.

Right. Manny saw his family hunted down by humans. How do you think that made him feel? Pause for and affirm answers.

I want each of you to think about a time someone did something wrong to you. Then take a crayon or two, and go over to our papered walls. Draw your own hieroglyphics that tell your story.

After about five minutes, encourage everyone to finish up. Those who have finished can take their seats and get ready for the movie to start again.

Say: **I see some pretty good stories on our walls. After the movie, we'll have a chance to talk about them and see how God wants us to deal with these stories in our lives.**

After everyone has settled in their seats, dim the lights, and pick up the movie where you paused it.

Closing Credits (14 minutes)

Say: **Turn to a parent or partner, and share with that person the situation you drew in your hieroglyphic and how you think God might want you to treat the person who's hurt you.**

While moviegoers are talking, turn the "Howling Wind" track back on (track 13). After a few minutes have passed, ask for several volunteers to share how they answered the question. Affirm their answers, then say: **We all have things for which we need to forgive others. Sometimes it's not easy to forgive those who do wrong things to us, especially people who *continue* to do wrong things. But God** is willing to forgive each one of us—including people we have a hard time forgiving. God wants us to show others the same love he shows us.

Let's go over to the hieroglyphics we drew on the wall and continue our story. I want you to keep drawing, showing how you think God would want you to treat the person who wronged you. Remember, he has forgiven every one of us, and God even let his own son die and take the punishment for our sins.

Encourage the children as they draw. After about five to seven minutes, have children finish up and go back to their seats.

Say: **Manny had every reason not to forgive the humans for what they did to his family, but he chose to forgive them and help the baby. God has forgiven each of us, even though it was for our sins that Jesus had to die. He loves us that much. We need to remember his love for us whenever it's time to forgive someone else.**

If you don't know about Jesus, I'll be glad to talk to you about him after we finish tonight. Just hang around and we'll talk.

That's our movie tonight—thanks and good night!

Additional Themes Illustrated by This Movie:

loyalty, perseverance, and unconditional love

In the Spotlight:

THE LION KING

G | GENERAL AUDIENCES
All Ages Admitted

1994, Walt Disney Pictures
Running time: 89 minutes

The Point: God helps us deal with problems.

Simba mistakenly believes he killed his father—a problem if ever there was one. As Simba explores ways to deal with guilt, your children will discover that God will help them deal with their problems.

The Passage: James 1:12

"Blessed is the man who perseveres under trial, because when he has stood the test, he will receive the crown of life that God has promised to those who love him."

Notes to the Director

The Lion King has a running time of 89 minutes, so you'll have 31 minutes to help children realize that God can help them deal with problems.

Environment

This movie takes place in Africa, where many of God's wonderful animals are represented. Help create a feel for this beautiful part of God's world by dressing in a bush hat and encouraging children to create a mural of African animals. Tape butcher paper to a wall for the mural, and place crayons or markers nearby. Be sure that the markers won't bleed through and stain the wall. If that's a problem, double or triple the pieces of paper.

Play the "African Animal Crossing" track of the *More Than a Movie* CD (track 14) as children arrive. Set your CD player on "repeat" so the track plays nonstop until the movie begins.

Many animals in Africa eat insects, and your kids will enjoy sweet gummy worm "grubs" for a snack.

Cautions

This movie contains several scenes that might frighten very young children. The fight between Scar and Mufasa near the beginning of the movie ultimately results in Mufasa's death. This scene may frighten and sadden many young children.

Another fight, this one between Scar and an adult Simba, occurs at the end of the movie.

Supplies

- CD player
- *More Than a Movie* CD
- white butcher paper
- tape
- markers or crayons
- gummy worms (two per participant)
- construction paper
- scissors
- stapler

Opening Credits (10 minutes)

Walk in front of the screen wearing a bush hat.

Say: **Welcome to our *More Than a Movie* night! We're screening *The Lion King*, a film about a young lion who has a lot of troubles.** Pause briefly, cup your hand around your ear, and pretend to listen to the animal sounds.

Listen! We must be near an animal crossing! I can hear lots of animal noises. Turn to someone sitting next to you, and see how many animals you can name that you might be hearing at this animal crossing. You have 20 seconds.

Ask for volunteers to suggest animals that might be responsible for the sounds they're hearing. Then encourage the participants to help you make an "Animal Crossing" sign by drawing animals they think they heard.

If children aren't sure what to do, suggest that they draw elephants, lions, monkeys, wart hogs, hyenas, giraffes, or parrots. Give children five minutes to complete their pictures, then ask them to put away the markers and return to their seats.

Say: **This movie reminds me that God can help us with our problems. We don't have to worry about problems—God will help us deal with whatever we face.**

Let's watch the movie to see what kinds of problems Simba, a young lion, encounters.

One more thing: During this movie, we'll hear a lot about young Simba becoming a king when he grows up. Every time you hear Simba say the word *king*, I want you to touch your fingertips together to form a circle—a crown—and place them on top of your head. Then say, "Hail, King Simba." Let's try it three times.

Say the word *king* three times, pausing each time for participants to place the "crowns" on top of their heads and then shout, "Hail, King Simba." Then close the Opening Credits by saying: **Now let's join the animals in Africa!**

Dim the lights and turn off the CD player as the movie begins.

Be prepared to start the intermission about 47 minutes into the film, when Timon, and Pumbaa, and a now-adult Simba finish singing the song "Hakuna Matata" and walk away together.

Intermission (10 minutes)

Once you've paused the movie, gradually turn the lights back on, and return to the front of the room.

Say: **Wow! A lot has happened to our young friend Simba. He thought he was** responsible for his father's death, and that made him incredibly sad—so sad, in fact, that he ran away from his family and friends.

In 10 minutes, we'll return to our movie to see what happens to Simba. Between now and then, feel free to take a bathroom break.

Join me in standing up, please. Let's play a game to remind us of all the animals we've seen in the movie so far.

First, lean over just a bit with your head facing the floor. Hold your arm in front of your face to make a long, long nose—we'll call it a "trunk." What animal do you think we look like? Right! An elephant! Let's walk like an elephant and swing our trunks. Pause while the children walk around the room pretending to be elephants.

Now let's use our other arm.

Stand up tall on tippy-toes, and stretch your arm way up above your head. That arm now looks like a long, long neck. Move your hand like a mouth opening and closing. Walk around on tippy-toes, pretending to eat the leaves out of tall trees. Which animal do you think we are? You've got it—we're giraffes! Pause while the children tiptoe around the room pretending to be giraffes.

Now let's be birds. Flap your arms as you move around the room, and decide which one of the birds in the movie you want to be. Pause while the children pretend to fly. Ask them the names of the birds they saw in the movie.

Now let's be Pumbaa—we're going to snort like a pig. Show the children how to position their hands to look like tusks, with the thumbs touching either side of their mouths, the next three fingers closed tight, and the pinkie curled outward. Encourage the children to snort like a pig while they walk around the room.

Boy, after watching the movie and pretending to be Pumbaa, I think I'm getting a little hungry. Is there anyone else out there who would like a nice, juicy grub for a snack? I'll share my grubs with you, and then it will almost be time for the movie to begin again.

As adult helpers pass out one gummy worm to each child, say: When we paused the movie, our friends had just finished a song featuring the phrase *hakuna matata*, which means "no worries."

There's a verse in the Bible that says, "Blessed is the man who perseveres"—that means a man who doesn't give up—"under trial, because when he has stood the test, he will receive the crown of life that God has promised to those who love him."

A man named James wrote that to remind people to keep believing in Jesus, even if they are having their share of troubles. Hakuna matata, James said—no worries. That's because if Christians keep believing and persevering, God gives them the crown of life. Then they get to be in heaven with God forever.

Let's finish our movie to see if Simba perseveres. If you'd like one more grub to enjoy during the show, raise your hand, and I'll toss you one!

After you distribute more snacks, ask moviegoers to settle in as you dim the lights and pick up the movie where you paused it.

Closing Credits (11 minutes)

Say: **While you're still thinking about the movie, quickly turn to a parent or friend, and tell that person which animal in the story was your favorite.**

After five seconds, say: **At first, Simba tried to run from his problems. Later, he faced his troubles and persevered—he didn't give up. Then he became the king of the animals.**

Being king of the animals is pretty cool, but God is the king of the whole *universe*. And just as the animals respected and listened to their king, we should listen to and serve *our* king, who is God. Why? Because God loves us and wants to help us deal with our problems.

We're going to make crowns to take home that will remind us that our heavenly Father and King helps us deal with problems.

Encourage children to use their creativity and the supplies provided (crayons, construction paper, and scissors) to make crowns. Ask adults to handle any stapling duties.

When you have just one minute left, ask children to put down the supplies, and say: **Put on your crowns. Now you're all kings of the animals! Of course, if a lion shows up to challenge you, you might want to resign your job!**

Simba got help so he could overcome his problems. We can get help, too— from God!

That's our movie tonight. Thanks and good night.

Additional Themes Illustrated by This Movie:

courage, family, friendship, and problems

In the Spotlight:

THE LITTLE MERMAID

G | GENERAL AUDIENCES
All Ages Admitted

1989, Walt Disney Pictures
Running Time:
83 minutes

The Point: Obey your parents.

A mermaid princess gets in trouble when she ignores her father's instructions. Your children will consider what happens when *they* disobey their parents.

The Passage: Ephesians 6:1

"Children, obey your parents in the Lord, for this is right."

Notes to the Director

The Little Mermaid has a running time of 83 minutes, so you'll have 37 minutes to help children understand the importance of obeying their parents.

Environment

Much of the movie takes place underwater, so play the "Ocean Sounds" track of the *More Than a Movie* CD (track 15) as children arrive. Set your CD player on "repeat" so the track plays nonstop until the movie begins.

Carry the theme through to the snacks by serving trail mix. Why would a mermaid need trail mix? She wouldn't—unless, like Ariel, she suddenly has legs instead of fins!

Set up the snack center and bubble center before children arrive, but keep supplies out of sight until the appropriate time.

Cautions

This movie contains several scenes that might frighten very young children. A large shark chases Ariel and Flounder near the beginning of the movie. Near the middle of the movie, when Ursula strikes a bargain with Ariel, she and her two eel cohorts are fairly menacing.

Also, near the end of the movie, Ursula grows both in size and in power and is intimidating.

Supplies

- CD player
- *More Than a Movie* CD
- bubble solution and wands
- tarp for the floor during bubble play
- Goldfish crackers
- Cheerios

- Chinese noodles
- miniature marshmallows
- raisins
- paper cups
- plastic spoons

Opening Credits (10 minutes)

Walk in front of the screen wearing a fishing vest and cap and carrying a fishing pole and fishnet.

Say: **Welcome to our *More Than a Movie* night! We're screening *The Little Mermaid*, a film about a mermaid who finds herself in a difficult situation when she disobeys her father.**

Turn to someone sitting next to you, and see how many sea creatures you can think of in 30 seconds. Go!

Ask for a show of hands to see how many sea creatures the pairs could name. Ask for volunteers to call out the animals they thought of.

Say: **Wow—there are a *lot* of animals in the ocean! I brought all of my fishing equipment to see if I could catch something, maybe even something really big like a whale or a mermaid.**

The list you gave me is great, but I'm not sure I'd recognize all those sea animals even if I caught one of them. So would you help me? Stand up, please, and when I call out an animal, impersonate it so I'll be able to recognize the animal if it ends up in my net.

Ask children to act out the following animals one at a time: lobster, clam, shark, sea horse, eel, octopus, whale, flying fish, and mermaid. Add other sea creatures if you wish, and encourage kids to look around to see how other children are impersonating these animals.

Say: **Thanks! I especially appreciate the mermaid impersonation because I've never seen one in the ocean before. And I'll bet you haven't, either. But you're about to see one on this screen!**

One more thing: Even though most of our movie takes place underwater, you'll see many scenes that include a large, friendly dog. Whenever you hear the dog bark, I want you to yell, "Here, Max." Let's try it three times.

Lead children and adults in shouting, "Here, Max!" three times, then close the Opening Credits by saying: **Now let's go for a swim!**

Dim the lights and turn off the CD player as the movie begins.

Be prepared to start the intermission about 46 minutes into the film, when Flounder carries Ariel, who has just made a bargain with Ursula and now has legs, to the surface of the water.

Intermission (17 minutes)

Once you've paused the movie, gradually turn the lights back on, and return to the front of the room.

Say: **Well, Ariel has certainly had an adventure, hasn't she? In about 15 minutes, we'll resume the movie, so this is a great time to take a bathroom break or venture to the centers in the back of the room. At the snack center, you can prepare a snack** that Ariel will need now that she has legs: trail mix!

Allow children to take part in the bubble center or snack center. Before sending them to the centers, explain what children will do at each one.

At the Bubble Center

Encourage children to use the bubble wands to blow bubbles while playing these games:

- **Bubble Breath:** Blow a bubble, and see if you can hold your breath until the bubble pops.
- **Big, Bigger, Biggest:** Blow bubbles, seeing how large a bubble you can create.
- **Catch Me If You Can:** Blow bubbles, and try to catch them on the wand without breaking them.

At the Snack Center

Instruct children to make trail mix by combining a spoonful of each of the following ingredients in a paper cup:

- flounder fishies (Goldfish crackers)
- water bubbles (Cheerios)
- seaweed (Chinese noodles)
- jellyfish (miniature marshmallows)
- baby eels (raisins)

When there are two minutes left before the movie resumes, encourage children to settle back down in front of the screen.

Say: **Ariel really got herself in a mess when she disobeyed her father, didn't she?**

There's a story in the Bible about a young man who disobeyed his father. Even though he had a good life at home with his family, this young man asked for money from his father and then left home to do things he shouldn't do. And just like Ariel, he eventually found himself in a mess! I'll tell you more about him after the movie.

Now let's watch and see what happens to Ariel next.

Pick up the movie where you paused it.

Closing Credits (10 minutes)

Say: **Ariel apologized to her father and asked for forgiveness. That's good, since she did something wrong. She shouldn't have disobeyed her father at all.**

Sometimes parents can be wrong or make mistakes. But God still wants us to obey our parents.

Read Ephesians 6:1 aloud.

Say: **During the intermission, I started telling you about a story Jesus told in the Bible. Jesus told us about a young man who got bored with living at home on a farm. He wanted to go have fun in a city, so the young man asked his dad for money and left home.**

Soon, the young man started to party and very quickly ran out of money. When his money was gone, so were his good-time buddies, so the young man

took the only job he could find: feeding pigs. It was a smelly, low-paying job.

The young man decided to go home and ask for a job on his dad's farm. That had to be a hard decision—the young man was coming back broke, hungry, and wearing rags. He'd left the farm rich and proud, but he wasn't proud anymore.

The young man started to apologize to his father, but his father said, "I'm glad you're home!" He forgave his son and threw a party to welcome the young man home.

That young man learned that disobeying his father and ignoring his dad's advice were dumb things to do. And he also learned just how much his father loved him.

While you're still thinking about the movie, quickly turn to a partner, and answer these questions:

• What's some advice you've gotten from your parents that turned out to be true?

• Why do you think it's a good idea to listen to and obey your parents?

Give pairs a few minutes to talk, then draw attention back to yourself.

Say: **It's hard to obey parents sometimes, isn't it? Well, it's hard to be a parent too. If you're a parent, please stand up. I want to pray for you.**

When parents are standing, pray: **Dear God, please use these parents to help their children grow up healthy and strong. Use these parents to encourage their children to know, love, and follow you. Amen.**

Ask children to stand, too, and pray for them: **Dear God, please help these children to obey their parents. Thank you for giving us people to help us grow up in ways that honor you. Thanks for parents. Amen.**

That's our movie tonight—thanks for coming and God bless you!

Additional Themes Illustrated by This Movie:

friendship, honesty, loyalty, and parents

In the Spotlight:

MONSTERS, INC.

G | GENERAL AUDIENCES
All Ages Admitted

2001, Pixar Animation
Studios and Walt Disney
Pictures
Running time: 92 minutes

The Point: God protects us.

Monsters who collect screams from human children in order to power the monsters' world accidentally come to love and protect a human child. Use this movie to help children think about how much God loves and protects them.

The Passage: Psalm 91:14-16

" 'Because he loves me,' says the Lord, 'I will rescue him; I will protect him, for he acknowledges my name. He will call upon me, and I will answer him; I will be with him in trouble, I will deliver him and honor him. With long life will I satisfy him and show him my salvation.' "

Notes to the Director

Monsters, Inc. has a running time of 92 minutes, so you'll have just 28 minutes to help children make the connection between how Sulley and Mike protect Boo and how God protects us.

Environment

Most of the action happens at or around the Monsters, Inc. factory, so create a factory theme. Place stacked boxes, safety cones, caution tape, and hard hats around the screening area. Be sure to play the "Scary Sounds" track of the *More Than a Movie* CD (track 16) as children arrive. Set your CD player on "repeat" so the track plays nonstop until the movie begins.

Carry the theme through to the snacks by serving "monsters" (Teddy Grahams).

Cautions

This movie is about monsters—odd and often funny monsters, but monsters just the same. There are some intense moments at the beginning and from time to time throughout the film that may scare younger children. Once they understand that the monsters are more silly than scary, you should be fine.

Supplies
- CD player
- *More Than a Movie* CD
- balloons (two for each student)
- permanent markers (one for every two students)
- stand-up inflatable punching bag

Opening Credits (10 minutes)

Walk in front of the screen wearing a hard hat and eye protection goggles. Carry a clipboard, and look through papers as you talk.

Say: **Welcome to our *More Than a Movie* night! We're screening *Monsters, Inc.*, a film about how love conquers fear. You'll meet a pretty strange group of creatures in our movie. Sometimes they're scary and sometimes they're funny, but they're always interesting!**

Ask several volunteers to make sure each person has a balloon.

Say: **If you're 7 years old or older, blow up your balloon, and tie it so it stays inflated. Then help the kids who are younger than 7 do the same with their balloons.**

When each person has an inflated balloon, share the markers I'll toss out to you. Use a marker to draw a monster face on your balloon. Then, somewhere on your balloon monster, write the answer to this question: "What scares you?" On my balloon, I'd write [a fear to which the children can relate].

A warning: These are permanent markers, so if you draw on your clothes, the marks won't come out! Parents, you may want to help your children draw.

Allow children to work with each other for several minutes.

Say: **Show your balloon monsters to the people around you. You can also share the thing you wrote down that scares you the most.** Give the children a minute or two to share as you collect markers.

Before we screen the movie, let me tell you about someone who loves and protects you. In the movie, you'll see how two really nice guys, who also happen to be monsters, meet and protect a little girl named Boo.

There's someone who wants to protect you, too. He's big enough and strong enough, and he's waiting for you to trust him. But we'll get to that later.

One more thing: If you watch the movie closely, you'll see a sock get stuck onto the back of one of the monsters. It will happen a couple of times. When you see the sock, I want you to yell, "That's gotta stink!"

Feeling afraid is just like a dirty sock. It stinks! Let's practice a couple of times. There's the sock!

Lead the children and adults in shouting, "That's gotta stink!" three times, then close the Opening Credits by saying: **Snuggle close to someone safe. Here come the monsters!**

Dim the lights and turn off the CD player as the movie begins.

Be prepared to start the intermission about 46 minutes into the film, when Mike's girlfriend, Celia, confronts him and you hear the line, "Sushi? Sushi? You think I care about sushi?"

Intermission (10 minutes)

Once you have paused the movie, gradually turn the lights back on, and return to the front of the room.

Say: **Now who was scared? I didn't think any of you were. In 10 minutes we'll start again, so this is a great time to take a bathroom break or get more snacks.**

During the break, take a moment to smack as you snack! We've got an inflated punching bag. Feel free to stop by and give it a smack. But as you do, you have to

say, "God protects me and can beat down any fear!"

Let children and parents punch on the bag and get snacks. When 10 minutes have passed, dim the lights, and pick up the movie where you paused it.

Closing Credits (8 minutes)

Say: **While you're still thinking about the movie, quickly turn to a parent or partner, and discuss this question:**

• **How did Sulley and Mike protect Boo? You've got one minute to talk.**

While moviegoers are talking, turn the "Scary Sounds" track back on (track 16).

After a minute has passed, ask for several volunteers to share how they answered the question. Affirm their answers, then say: **When you care about someone, as Sulley cared about Boo, you want to protect that person.**

God feels the same way about you. He loves you so much that even in scary times, you can know without a doubt that God is with you and will protect you.

When you have to face your **monsters, whatever they are, God will never let you face them alone. He'll always be there.**

It's true that you may have to wrestle with your fears, and they may go away for a while and then come back. But God will never leave you alone. He will always come alongside you when you face your fears.

You made a balloon monster when you came in and wrote one of your fears on that monster. Gather in groups of three or four, and share with your group how you think God can protect you from the fear you've written on your balloon monster.

Give groups three minutes to talk.

Say: **Remember, God is bigger than any fear, and God is strong enough to protect you from anything!**

Let's pray together about God helping us when we're afraid. I'll say a prayer out loud, and if you agree with what I'm saying, repeat the words out loud.

Dear God (pause), **sometimes things scare us.** (Pause.) **Sometimes people scare us.** (Pause.) **But we know that you love us and will protect us.** (Pause.) **Help us to depend on you** (pause), **and when we're scared** (pause), **help us to trust in you.** (Pause.)

Lord, never let us forget (pause) **that you promised to be with us** (pause) **everywhere and all the time.** (Pause.) **Amen.**

If you said that prayer, then your fears aren't as scary as you once thought they were. So here's what I want you to do. If you believe that God is big enough, and if you believe that God is strong enough, and if you know in your heart that, compared to God, anything that scares you is weak and silly, I want you to pop your monster balloon on the count of three!

Don't worry. I'll give you a new clean balloon with no fears written on it to take home. But now I want you to see how God can explode even your worst fears. Ready? One, two, three!

Show children how to sit on their balloons to break them. Do not demonstrate how to break a balloon by stamping on it—that's guaranteed to twist some child's ankle!

Say: **If you'd like to talk more about how God protects you, I'll be glad to talk with you. Just hang around, and we'll talk.**

That's our movie tonight—thanks and good night!

Additional Themes Illustrated by This Movie:

courage, good and evil, and love

MULAN

G | GENERAL AUDIENCES
All Ages Admitted

1998, Walt Disney Pictures
Running time: 88 minutes

The Point: God gives us gifts to use for serving others.

A woman serving in the Chinese army uses her gifts and skills to become a hero. Your children will consider how they can use their gifts and skills to serve God.

The Passage: Romans 12:6-8

"We have different gifts, according to the grace given us. If a man's gift is prophesying, let him use it in proportion to his faith. If it is serving, let him serve; if it is teaching, let him teach; if it is encouraging, let him encourage; if it is contributing to the needs of others, let him give generously; if it is leadership, let him govern diligently; if it is showing mercy, let him do it cheerfully."

Notes to the Director

Mulan has a running time of 88 minutes, so you'll have a little more than 30 minutes to help children understand that we can use the gifts and talents God has given us to serve each other.

Environment

This movie takes place in China, with most of the scenes in an army camp, so create your own Chinese army camp. You can hang paper lanterns and put up a small tent in the corner of the room.

Outside the tent, set up a small table with scratch paper, pencils, and a basket for the opening activity. And be sure to play the "Drumbeat and Gong" track of the *More Than a Movie* CD (track 17) as children arrive. Set your CD player on "repeat" so the track plays nonstop until the movie begins. When children come in, give them each a piece of paper and pencil.

Carry the theme through to the snacks by serving rice cakes. Consider having several flavors of rice cakes available.

Cautions

This movie contains battle scenes where soldiers fight one another, which might frighten very young children.

Supplies

- CD player
- *More Than a Movie* CD
- rice cakes (at least two per child)
- scratch paper

- pencils
- small table
- basket

Opening Credits (7 minutes)

Say: **Welcome to our *More Than a Movie* night! We're screening *Mulan*, a film about a young Chinese girl who joins the Chinese army and finds that her gifts and skills help make her a hero.**

We'll watch Mulan discover that she can do things she never thought possible!

When you came in, you got a piece of paper and a pencil. Think of a silly talent you have that most people don't know about, such as touching your nose with your tongue or singing the alphabet backwards. Write your talent and your name on your piece of paper. Then fold up the paper, and put it in the basket by our tent. You have one minute. Go!

Remind kids to put their names on the papers so you know who has which talent. Tell kids that there will be a talent show during the intermission. At the talent show, you'll read the pieces of paper, and the kids will guess who has which talent. Ask kids who don't mind demonstrating their talent to each put a star on their paper. Only call on children who have put stars on their papers.

During the first part of the movie, read through the papers, and choose a few to read during the intermission. Be sure to choose only ones that have stars on them.

Say: **This movie reminds me that we've all been given gifts of different skills and talents that we can use to help those around us. Sometimes we're able to help others in pretty amazing ways.**

Before we screen the movie, I want those of you who've ever received a gift of any kind to raise your hand.

You'll probably see every hand raised.

Say: **I thought so. We've all received gifts. Now raise your hand if you were given a gift but then told you couldn't use it. You were to put it away, forget about it, and let it gather dust.**

No hands up? That's not a surprise.

It would be silly to give someone a gift that couldn't ever be used. When we receive a gift, we want to use it!

The Apostle Paul wrote a letter about gifts to the Christians in Rome. Paul said that we all have talents and skills we can use to help each other and to glorify God. He said we should encourage people to use their gifts.

As we watch this movie, notice that Mulan uses her gifts and skills to help her people. And notice that she isn't encouraged to use her gifts!

Whenever you see Mulan do something that Chinese girls weren't supposed to do, say, "Girls rule!" This may be hard for some of you boys to say, but see if you can do it. Let's practice three times.

Lead children and adults in practicing, then dim the lights and turn off the CD player as the movie begins.

Be prepared to start the movie about 52 minutes into the film, when Mulan lays a doll by a sword right after the captain says, "We're the only hope for the emperor. Now move out!"

Intermission (15 minutes)

Once you have paused the movie, gradually turn the lights back on, and return to the front of the room.

Say: **What an adventure! In about 15 minutes we'll resume, so this is a great time to take a bathroom break or get another rice cake.**

Before we start our talent show, let's all stand up and do a little marching exercise like soldiers.

Lead everyone in a quick Follow the Leader-type game while marching. Let those who need to use the restroom march to the restroom. As you march, stretch your arms, and help the children get the wiggles out. After two or three minutes of marching, get everyone back to their seats.

Say: **When you came in today, you wrote down a talent you have. Let's see if we can guess who our talented friends are.**

One at a time, read aloud the slips of paper you chose. Do as many as you have time for, and be sure to ask only the children who've put stars on their papers to demonstrate their talents.

After about 12 minutes, say: **We have some uniquely talented people here. Thank you, all you performers! Let's give them a big hand.** Lead the group in applause.

Ask your moviegoers to settle in, dim the lights, and pick up the movie where you paused it.

Closing Credits (10 minutes)

Say: **While you're still thinking about the movie, quickly turn to a parent or partner, and discuss this question:**

• **What was the greatest talent or gift that Mulan used to defeat her enemies?**

While moviegoers talk, play the "Drumbeat and Gong" track (track 17). After one minute, ask for volunteers to share how they answered the question.

Affirm their answers, then say: **It's great that Mulan was able to use her gifts to save her army and her family. She knew she had a lot to offer, and when people let her use her gifts, everyone benefited.**

Turn to your partner again. Talk about how you could use your talents to help others and to glorify God. Remember that things you like to do are often things that show your talents.

Here are some examples: Maybe you're good at drawing. You could create artwork to share with the residents of a retirement home. Or maybe you're good at soccer. You could help someone who's not quite as good and, in the process, make a new friend who you could invite to church.

Whatever your gift is, God has given it to you for a purpose. He didn't give it to you to just tuck away and never use. God wants us to use our gifts to help others.

If you aren't sure if you know God and what he wants for your life, I'll be glad to talk to you. Just hang around after the movie, and we can talk.

That's our movie tonight—thanks and good night!

Additional Themes Illustrated by This Movie:

courage, loyalty, perseverance, and prejudice

OLIVER & COMPANY

The Point: Put others first.

A crew of New York City animals puts others first…and your children will explore how they can do the same thing.

G **GENERAL AUDIENCES**
All Ages Admitted

1988, Walt Disney Pictures
Running time: 72 minutes

The Passage: Philippians 2:1-4

"If you have any encouragement from being united with Christ, if any comfort from his love, if any fellowship with the Spirit, if any tenderness and compassion, then make my joy complete by being like-minded, having the same love, being one in spirit and purpose. Do nothing out of selfish ambition or vain conceit, but in humility consider others better than yourselves. Each of you should look not only to your own interests, but also to the interests of others."

Notes to the Director

Oliver & Company has a running time of 72 minutes, which will give you 48 minutes to make the connection between the generosity of Oliver and his friends and Jesus' generosity, which we can reflect and live out with people we encounter daily. We can put others first too!

Environment

This movie takes place in New York City. Give your space a city feel by using the sketch pictured below as a template to create a backdrop of a city skyline.

Use butcher paper painted black to create the stylized skyscrapers, and hang them on the wall of your "screening room." Another option is to use cardboard to create the skyscraper outlines. Mount the cardboard so children walk past it as they enter the room.

CAUTION

Puppy Chow

2 cups chocolate chips

one 15-ounce box Crispix or Rice Chex cereal

1 cup peanut butter

½ cup margarine

3 cups confectioners' sugar

Heat chocolate chips, peanut butter, and margarine in a glass bowl in the microwave until melted. Mix well.

Combine cereal and chocolate mix. Stir until completely coated. Place confectioners' sugar in a bag, add cereal mix, and shake to coat.

Spread on wax paper. Let stand until set.

Serves 10.

Note: While this is a fun people snack, it should never be served to actual dogs! Also, be sure to provide an alternate snack for anyone with a nut allergy.

Create an obstacle course for children to go through during the intermission. Children will have their wrists tied together. Obstacles could include creating a card "tent" by leaning playing cards together so they stand upright, hitting spoons together behind the pair's back at least 10 times in a row, tossing a coin back and forth five times in a row and catching it on the back of one person's hand, putting nail polish on each other's thumbnails, and pouring a glass of water into an empty glass.

Create other challenges by using materials you have on hand that work in the space you have available.

Be sure to play the "City Sounds" track of the *More Than a Movie* CD (track 18) as children arrive. Set your CD player on "repeat" so the track plays nonstop until the movie begins.

Want to have even more fun? Borrow several very friendly, very housebroken dogs, and have them in open cages or a side-room petting zoo. Because some children may have allergies, it's important to put the dogs (or cats!) in an area away from where moviegoers have to sit.

Since most of the main characters in this movie are dogs, serve "puppy chow" as a snack (see recipe in margin). Be sure to have plenty of napkins or paper towels on hand!

Cautions

This movie contains a few scenes that may frighten very young children. Early in the movie, a few snarling, angry dogs chase Oliver, and Sykes and his dogs threaten Fagan and the animals. The scenes are brief, and no one is badly hurt.

Supplies

- CD player
- *More Than a Movie* CD
- ingredients for puppy chow (listed in recipe)
- small disposable plates for puppy chow
- napkins or paper towels
- orange flagging tape (found at home supply stores) cut into two-foot lengths
- items for the obstacle course (see above)

Opening Credits (10 minutes)

Walk in front of the screen wearing a leather jacket, leather pants or jeans, boots, sunglasses, and your best "cool dude" attitude.

Say: **Hey there, youse guys and gals! Welcome to our *More Than a Movie* night! Tonight we're gonna check out *Oliver & Company*, a movie about some cool cats and dogs in New York City!**

In the movie, we'll meet Oliver, a lonely kitten who's befriended by a group of "hoodlum" dogs. We'll also see lots of examples of people and animals putting others first. Let's do some lineups to see who's first in line.

Have kids line up against one wall. Then have them quickly rearrange themselves from left to right by height, with the shortest person at the far left end of the line. Then have them quickly line up alphabetically by the first letter of their first names, then by the last letter of their middle names. Then have them line up by birthplace with the person born furthest east at the beginning of the line.

This is most fun when there's a mad scramble, so encourage speed, and don't wait until one line is completely formed before launching the next challenge.

Have everyone sit back down.

Say: **This game made it easy to figure out who was first in line. It reminds me of someone who put others first a lot.**

Many people who met this person considered him a king—someone to be worshipped and held in high regard. But he lived his life for other people, wanting to save them and help them. He fed their hungry souls and their hungry bodies.

One time, he sat down to eat with a group of close friends who traveled with him. After they ate together, he did something that *amazed* **the people he was with. He…well, I'll tell you about that at the end of the movie.**

Do you all have your snacks? We'll have an intermission near the middle of the movie, and that will be the time to load up on more snacks and take a bathroom break.

One more thing: During this movie, you'll hear several references to being "streetwise," having "street savoir-faire," or having "street smarts." Whenever you hear these phrases, I want you to do your best tough-guy imitation by putting your thumbs up and saying "Aaay!" Let's practice that a few times.

Lead children and adults in their best tough-guy imitations, then close the opening credits by saying: **Now let's go meet Oliver and his friends!**

Dim the lights and turn off the CD player as the movie begins. Be prepared to start the intermission after about 36 minutes, when everyone goes to sleep.

Intermission (18 minutes)

Once you've paused the movie, gradually turn the lights back on, and return to the front of the room.

Say: **Wow—what a cool movie! In about 15 minutes, we'll start the movie again, so this is a great time to take a bathroom break or get some more puppy chow.**

Let's play a fun game! First you'll need to find a partner. Then come and get a length of flagging tape. Use the flagging tape to carefully tie one of your wrists to one of your partner's wrists. If you need help, let me know.

After partners are attached to each other, say: **Now we're going to see how well you and your partner can work together. I've set up a course full of fun challenges for you to complete with your partner.**

Take a few moments to quickly demonstrate each challenge to participants. When everyone understands the tasks, have the first pair begin the course. Once the first pair has finished the first task, start the next pair. If children break the flagging tape (it's easy to do!), have them get another piece and start the obstacle course over.

Once all pairs have finished, have the group give themselves a big "Aaay!" for being so street-smart!

If there's still time before the intermission ends, let kids relax and talk together. When the 15 minutes have passed, ask moviegoers to settle in, dim the lights, and begin the movie where you paused it.

Closing Credits (20 minutes)

Say: **OK, you cool cats! While you've still got the movie in your head, quickly find a partner, and discuss this question:**

- **Who in the movie put someone else first—and in what ways?**

Ask for volunteers to share their insights.

Say: **Isn't it great that all these characters looked beyond their own needs and wants and thought of someone else first? These characters sacrificed for each other.**

When someone makes a sacrifice for someone else, it means that the person gives up something important in order to bring joy, peace, or comfort to someone else.

Earlier I said that a king did something amazing for his friends one evening after dinner. He did something that only the lowest servants did: He washed their feet.

His friends wore sandals and had dirty feet from walking on dusty streets. Usually a servant washed the feet of dinner guests. But this king took a towel and basin of water and went around the table, gently washing each of his friends' feet.

Some of the king's friends were shocked: They didn't think such a great man should be seen doing something servants do.

But the king insisted, so King Jesus washed their feet. Then he walked out of the room to serve in an even greater way: He died on the cross to pay for the sins of his friends. He paid for *our* sins too.

Let's think of some ways we can follow Jesus' example in our own lives. With your partner, think of one way you could put someone else's needs above your own.

For example, maybe you'll let someone else go first in line at the store. Or maybe you'll give up some hanging-out time to help a parent paint a room or clean out a basement. Think of something, then decide how you and your partner could act out your idea. You've got three minutes to come up with the idea and to decide how to act it out. Go!

After three minutes have passed, ask each pair to join another pair. Have each pair act out its idea for putting others first. The pair watching will guess what the action was and who was helped. If you have less than 10 pairs, consider having pairs act out their service ideas in front of the entire group.

After both pairs have had a chance to act out their actions, gather everyone together again.

Say: **Thanks for sharing in the fun times tonight! If you'd like to know more about Jesus and his sacrifice for us, feel free to hang around and chat.**

Have a great night!

Additional Themes Illustrated by This Movie:

courage, friendship, redemption, and selflessness

PINOCCHIO

The Point: Make choices that please God.

A wooden marionette learns how to make wise choices…and your kids will too.

G | GENERAL AUDIENCES
All Ages Admitted

1940, Walt Disney Pictures
Running time: 88 minutes

The Passage: Colossians 3:12-14

"Therefore, as God's chosen people, holy and dearly loved, clothe yourselves with compassion, kindness, humility, gentleness and patience. Bear with each other and forgive whatever grievances you may have against one another. Forgive as the Lord forgave you. And over all these virtues put on love, which binds them all together in perfect unity."

Notes to the Director

Pinocchio has a running time of 88 minutes, which will give you 32 minutes to make the connection between Pinocchio's choices—both good and bad—and the choices your students make.

Environment

A significant part of this movie focuses on Pinocchio's performance as a marionette, so create a performance space by setting up a stage.

Place shop lights with colored light bulbs along the floor to create a stage lighting effect. Be sure to have the "Applause" track of the *More Than a Movie* CD (track 20) cued up for use.

Continue the marionette theme by serving string licorice as a snack.

Cautions

This movie contains one line that refers to a character as a "jackass." The character has turned into a donkey, but the modern use of the word may cause this reference to raise a few eyebrows.

Supplies

- CD player
- *More Than a Movie* CD
- string licorice
- ball of string or yarn
- face paint
- 3x5 card and pen for signing an autograph

Opening Credits (10 minutes)

Just before you walk out on stage, start the "Applause" track of the *More Than a Movie* CD (track 20). Walk out with strings tied to your hands and feet and your face painted like a marionette. If you want to *really* go all out, add backstage panels, and have someone on a riser behind the panels to hold your strings.

Wave to the kids as if you're greeting admiring fans, bow slightly, and use a pen to sign an autograph for a child. The applause lasts 30 seconds and then fades.

Say: **Greetings, fellow puppets! Welcome to our *More Than a Movie* night! Tonight we'll watch *Pinocchio*, a movie about a wooden marionette, or puppet, named Pinocchio who wants to be a real boy. Pinocchio faces many choices in his quest to be real—we'll see how he handles these choices.**

Let's begin by pretending to be marionettes.

Ask kids to stand up and form pairs. Ask the person in each pair who has the longest shoelaces to be the puppeteer first. The other member of each pair will be the puppet.

Say: **Puppeteers control marionettes by holding the strings tied to their arms and legs. When a puppeteer raises his left thumb, for instance, the puppet's left arm goes up. Give that a try, puppeteers. Let's see if your puppets respond.**

Very good!

Now try your right thumb—your puppet's right arm should go up.

Now try your right little finger—your puppet's right leg should go up.

Now try your left little finger—your puppet's left leg should go up.

Now, puppeteers, take 30 seconds to get your puppets moving around!

After the 30 seconds are up, have members of each pair shift roles for another 30 seconds.

Then have pairs sit down to discuss the following questions:

• **What was it like to be the puppeteer? What did you like about it? dislike?**

• **What was it like to be the marionette? What did you like about it? dislike?**

Say: **It would be pretty difficult to have someone else holding strings and controlling your actions and choices all the time, wouldn't it? Of course, that would mean you wouldn't have to make your own decisions, either. Pinocchio wanted to make his own decisions, even though that can be hard sometimes. We'll see what sort of choices he made once he got the chance.**

Do you all have your snacks? We'll have an intermission in about an hour, and that will be the time to load up on more snacks and take a bathroom break.

One more thing: During this movie, you'll hear characters whistle from time to time. When you hear a whistle, I want you to shout out, "Let your conscience be your guide!" Let's practice that a few times.

Lead children and adults in shouting, "Let your conscience be your guide!" a few times, then close the Opening Credits by saying: **Now let's meet *Pinocchio*!**

Dim the lights and turn off the CD player as the movie begins. Be prepared to start the intermission about 54 minutes into the film, after Pinocchio and Jiminy Cricket escape Stromboli's carriage and run away into the night.

Intermission (15 minutes)

Once you've paused the movie, gradually turn the lights back on, and return to the front of the room.

Say: **Wow—what a cool movie! In about 15 minutes, we'll start the movie again, so this is a great time to take a bathroom break or get some more licorice.**

Let's play a couple of fun games now.

Have kids gather in a circle. Step into the circle, and say: **We're going to do some simple marionette motions together—kind of like "marionette aerobics." I'll begin by doing a simple motion. I want you all to imitate me. Then I'll point to someone, and** *that* **person will take my place in the center of the circle. He or she will demonstrate a different motion that we'll all imitate, then that person point to someone else. We'll continue until everyone has had a chance to lead.**

Stand in the center, and begin with a simple motion such as touching your nose or touching your toes. Be sure to imitate the jerky, stiff movements of a marionette. After a few seconds, point to someone else in the circle. When everyone has had a chance, say: **I think that was too easy for sharp marionettes like you. Let's go around the circle again, but this time, each person has to do all the actions that were demonstrated in this round plus add a new one. Ready?**

Start the round, then step back into the circle so you can play along. When the round is over, have kids sit down in a circle.

Say: **So far in the movie, we've seen Pinocchio and others make some good choices and some not-so-good choices. We're going to talk about some of these choices, as well as some choices we make in our own lives.**

Let's begin with the *not*-**so-good choices.**

I have a ball of yarn here. I'm going to hold it by one end and toss it to someone in the circle. As I toss it, I'm going to say one of the bad choices Pinocchio made or a bad choice I've seen someone make in real life. The person who catches the ball will hold onto the strand and then toss the rest of the ball to someone else while stating another bad choice.

Continue in this way until everyone has had a chance to toss the yarn and state a bad choice.

Say: **Wow. Look at this tangled mess we've made! This is kind of like what happens when we make bad choices—we end up in a tangle. Let's see if we can undo this mess with some good choices.**

Reverse the process, this time stating either *good* choices Pinocchio made or good choices people have made in their own lives.

Once the yarn has been returned to you, whistle once, and have the group shout out, "Let your conscience be your guide!" Then ask moviegoers to settle in. Dim the lights, and begin the movie where you paused it.

Closing Credits (20 minutes)

Say: **While you've still got the movie in your head, quickly discuss these questions with a person sitting next to you:**

- **What happened as a result of Pinocchio's bad choices?**
- **What happened as a result of Pinocchio's good choices?**

Say: **Pinocchio got his wish—he wasn't tied with strings. There was no puppeteer controlling him, so Pinocchio had to figure out what to do on his own. But Pinocchio wasn't *really* alone. Jiminy Cricket acted as his conscience, a little voice to help Pinocchio know right from wrong.**

There are no strings on us, either. We get to make choices every day.

God wants us to make good choices—choices that honor him. But God doesn't *make* us choose good things. We're not puppets. God wants us to choose to honor him because we love him, not because he's bigger than us.

We don't have to make all the choices alone, just as Pinocchio wasn't stuck making his choices alone. We have the Bible to tell us what some smart decisions are. We also have pastors, teachers, and parents to help us make good choices.

And we have our consciences, too. True, our consciences don't look like bugs, and they don't break into song, but if we love God and want to please him, our consciences and the Holy Spirit will guide us in that direction.

To help you remember what you've learned this evening about making good choices, I'd like to give each of you a piece of string.

Distribute a length of string to each moviegoer. Ask kids to form foursomes and discuss the following question:

• **What can you do with this piece of string to help you make good choices?**

Encourage foursomes to brainstorm as many possible uses for the string as they can, then ask for volunteers to share what they discussed in their foursomes. Take your time with this; five to seven minutes isn't too long. Affirm answers and ideas.

Say: **When I look at this string, I'm reminded that, in many ways, "I've got no strings on me." Like Pinocchio, I can make choices. But I want them to be choices that please God because I love God and want to be in a friendship with him.**

If you feel that way too, have a friend help you tie your string around your finger. Let it remind you that God cares about every choice you make and wants you to make choices that please him.

In your foursomes, discuss these questions:

• **What's a choice you could make this week that would please God?**
• **What's a choice you've made lately that you *don't* think pleased God?**

After foursomes have talked for a few minutes, draw attention back to yourself.

Say: **I wish I could say that all my choices are good choices, but I can't. Sometimes I do dumb things. Sometimes I make choices that don't please God. We all do.**

So let's do this: Let's ask God to forgive us for making choices that didn't please him. Let's apologize to God. He loves us and will forgive us if we do that.

In your foursomes, please share quick sentence prayers out loud. I'll close in about 30 seconds.

After 30 seconds, briefly pray aloud. Ask God to forgive you for the poor choices you've made, and affirm your love for God. Thank him for his love for you.

End by saying: **Thanks for sharing in our fun time tonight! If you'd like to know more about God's love and how you can make choices that please him, hang around, and we'll chat.**

Have a great night!

Additional Themes Illustrated by This Movie:

courage, lying, peer pressure, and truth

TARZAN

The Point: You have a place in the family of God.

Raised by gorillas, Tarzan has to decide where he truly belongs: with gorillas or with people. Use this movie to help your children see that they belong in the family of God!

G | GENERAL AUDIENCES
All Ages Admitted

1999, Walt Disney Pictures
Running time: 88 minutes

The Passage: 1 John 3:1

"How great is the love the Father has lavished on us, that we should be called children of God! And that is what we are!"

Notes to the Director

Tarzan has a running time of 88 minutes, so you'll have 32 minutes to help children make the connection between Tarzan's longing for family and God welcoming all of us into his family!

Environment

This movie takes place in the jungle, so create a jungle theme. Hang green crepe paper in a hallway or a doorway so children brush through it as they enter the room where you'll screen the movie. And be sure to play the "Jungle" track of the *More Than a Movie* CD (track 21) as children arrive. Set your CD player on "repeat" so the track plays nonstop until the movie begins.

Carry the theme through to the snacks by serving animal crackers.

Cautions

This movie contains several scenes that might be upsetting to very young children. A baby gorilla is attacked and carried away by a tiger.

Also, in the closing 10 minutes, the poacher Clayton shoots the gorilla leader, Kerchak. Clayton and Tarzan then fight. As he falls from a tree, Clayton gets entangled in vines, resulting in his death by hanging. Though shown in shadow, his suspended, swinging body is visible. Tarzan returns to the dying Kerchak, who utters his final words.

Supplies

- CD player
- *More Than a Movie* CD
- animal crackers
- disposable bowls for crackers

Opening Credits (5 minutes)

Walk in front of the screen wearing a safari hat and a bandanna draped around your neck. Remove the bandanna, and use it to wipe your face as if you're very warm.

Say: **Whew! It gets *hot* here in the jungle! I think it'd be a good idea for us to rest a while and watch a movie, don't you?**

Welcome to our *More Than a Movie* night! We're screening *Tarzan*, a film about a boy raised by gorillas. When he gets older, Tarzan has to decide whether he should remain in the jungle with his animal friends or leave the jungle to live with people.

Turn to someone sitting next to you, and discuss this question:

• Would you rather live in a house with people or in a jungle full of wild animals, and why? You've got 20 seconds.

Ask for a show of hands to see how many people would like to live in a house. Then ask for a show of hands to see how many would like to live in a jungle with wild animals.

Say: **Wow! It looks like some of you will be moving to the jungle soon! You know, the thing I care about the *most* when it comes to living somewhere is this: I want my family with me. I get lonely without my family!**

But sometimes people have to live away from their families. Maybe you have an older brother in college or an older sister in the army who lives far away from your family. That can be sad for us.

But here's good news: We're a family, too! Christians are all members of God's family because God is our Father. That makes all of us brothers and sisters!

And, unlike Tarzan, none of *our* brothers and sisters looks like a gorilla... right?

Do you all have your snacks? We're eating animal crackers because a lot of these animals, such as the lions and tigers, live in the jungle.

We'll have an intermission in about an hour. That will be the time to load up again on snacks and take a bathroom break.

One more thing: Several times during the movie, you'll hear the line, "In my heart." Each time we hear that line, let's point upwards to show that it is God who lives in *our* hearts. Let's practice. I'll say, "In my heart," and what will you do?

Rehearse the action with children several times. Then say: **Great job! Now let's watch *Tarzan* and see what he learns about the meaning of family!**

Dim the lights and turn off the CD player as the movie begins.

Be prepared to start the intermission about 45 minutes into the film, when Tarzan and Jane exchange names. Suddenly, gunshots ring out. Jane realizes that it is Clayton making the sound, and Tarzan and Jane swing off to meet up with him. Pause the movie as this scene ends.

Intermission (19 minutes)

Once you have paused the movie, gradually turn the lights back on, and return to the front of the room.

Say: **What an adventure! In several minutes we'll resume, so this is a great time to take a bathroom break or get another bowl of animal crackers.**

Join me in standing up, please. We're going to play a game while we take our intermission.

The first game is designed to get participants who've been seated a long time stretching and moving…but don't tell them that!

Say: **The first game is called In the Jungle. We saw lots of things in the jungle, didn't we? Let's take a quick tour. Do what I do.**

We saw really big trees with limbs that reached high into the sky! Reach up to the sky like a tree. Stretch your arms up in the air. **And those trees were covered with thousands of leaves!** Wiggle your fingers.

There were vines, too. Bend over at the waist, dangling your arms downward.

There were tigers in the jungle. Any tigers here in *our* jungle? Put your hands near your face in a claw position, and bare your teeth as if you're going to bite someone.

And there were elephants! Tarzan saw *lots* of elephants in the jungle! Bend over at the waist, dangle your arms toward the ground, and clasp your hands together to represent an elephant's trunk. **Elephants often walk slowly. Can you walk like an elephant?** Demonstrate an elephant walk.

Good job! Did we forget any of the animals we saw in the movie? Did we forget anything? Gorillas! I forgot the gorillas! How did the gorillas act? Step back—the response to this animal will be energetic!

Invite children to join you in applauding their efforts.

Say: **Remember when Tarzan put his hand up to the hand of Kala, his gorilla mother? Tarzan was looking for things about himself that were like his mother.**

Get in groups of three and discuss these questions:
• **In what ways do you *look* like your family?**
• **In what ways do you *act* like your family?**
• **In what ways are you *different* from your family?**

Allow one or two minutes for each question. Wrap up by saying: **We're often a lot like our families—but not *exactly* like them. God makes each of us special in unique ways.**

Whether we're a lot like our families or very different, the good news is that we have a place in a family. That family is the family of God.

God wants you to be in his forever family. He has a special spot for you to serve there. You belong in God's family, and joining it is as easy as telling God that you want to be a member. I can tell you more about that if you'd like after the movie.

Hey! It's time to watch the rest of the movie, so everyone crawl, hop, swing, or walk back to your seats. Let's see what happens next!

Dim the lights, and pick up the movie where you paused it.

Closing Credits (8 minutes)

Say: **While you're still thinking about the movie, quickly turn to a parent or partner and discuss these questions:**

• **How is Tarzan's family like or unlike your family? You've got one minute to talk.**

• **What's the most important thing Tarzan learned about family? You've got** one minute to talk.

While moviegoers are talking, turn the "Jungle" track back on (track 21). After each question, ask for several volunteers to share how they answered the question, and affirm their answers. After the second question, say: **Tarzan learned that family is partly about heart.**

We may not look exactly like other people in our family or even know who our birth parents are, but if we're loved, then we're part of a family. Tarzan's mom said that they were just the same in here (tap your chest).

That's how it is in God's family. God says that we're in his heart because he loves us so very much. And we can choose to love him, too. We can be in a growing relationship with him.

If you don't know about God, I'd be glad to talk to you about him after we finish tonight. Just hang around, and we'll talk.

That's our movie tonight—thanks and good night!

Additional Themes Illustrated by This Movie:

courage, fitting in, friendship, and loyalty

TOY STORY

The Point: Jealousy is dangerous.

A jealous toy does everything he can to remove a rival. Use this movie to help children discover how to grow past jealousy and make new friends.

The Passage: Genesis 4:3-9

"In the course of time Cain brought some of the fruits of the soil as an offering to the Lord. But Abel brought fat portions from some of the firstborn of his flock. The Lord looked with favor on Abel and his offering, but on Cain and his offering he did not look with favor. So Cain was very angry, and his face was downcast.

"Then the Lord said to Cain, 'Why are you angry? Why is your face downcast? If you do what is right, will you not be accepted? But if you do not do what is right, sin is crouching at your door; it desires to have you, but you must master it.'

"Now Cain said to his brother Abel, 'Let's go out to the field.' And while they were in the field, Cain attacked his brother Abel and killed him.

"Then the Lord said to Cain, 'Where is your brother Abel?'

" 'I don't know,' he replied. 'Am I my brother's keeper?' "

G | **GENERAL AUDIENCES**
All Ages Admitted

1995, Pixar Animation Studios and Walt Disney Pictures
Running time: 81 minutes

Notes to the Director

Toy Story has a running time of 81 minutes. That gives you almost 40 minutes to help kids make the connection between Woody's jealousy toward Buzz Light-year and the danger of jealousy in their own lives—and to help them turn that jealousy into friendship.

Environment

Set up your meeting area to look like a toy room or toy-filled bedroom. Borrow as many toys as you can from the nursery, preschool classes, and other church rooms. Ask parents if you can borrow their kids' toys. Here's another idea that could support a short-term mission project: Suggest that each family that attends brings a toy to donate.

Also be sure to play the "Toy Time" track on the *More Than a Movie* CD (track 22) as children arrive. Set your CD player on "repeat" so the track plays nonstop.

Part of the movie takes place at "Pizza Planet," so serve pizza or pizza-flavored chips.

Cautions

Toy Story has only a couple of scenes that might frighten young children. Woody knocks Buzz out of the window, Sid's vicious dog shows up a few times, and Sid's room features some scary toys and a few frights in the first four minutes of that scene. All of these scenes are brief, and no one gets hurt.

Supplies

- CD player
- *More Than a Movie* CD
- disposable plates and cups
- pizza slices or pizza-flavored chips
- juice or water
- one roll of toilet paper for every two moviegoers

Opening Credits (7 minutes)

Carry a massive armful of toys to the front of the room.

Say: **Welcome to our *More Than a Movie* night! We're screening a great movie about an adventure: *Toy Story*! On this adventure, we're going to Andy's room, to Sid's scary room, to Pizza Planet, and to infinity and beyond!**

I've brought some of my favorite toys with me. Turn to someone sitting next to you, and tell that person about *your* favorite toy. Where did you get your favorite toy? What's your toy's name, if it has one? And why is it your favorite? You each have one minute.

Give kids about two minutes to talk with their partners. About halfway through the discussion, signal when it's time to switch. Then ask for volunteers to share with everyone about their favorites.

Say: **Most of us have a favorite toy. But did you ever think about how toys feel when they're the favorite—and when they're not? In this movie, we find out how toys feel and how one toy's jealousy becomes a dangerous thing for himself and for all the other toys too.**

In a little while, we'll also hear about two brothers who also had a problem with jealousy. I'll tell you about that when we take a break.

Make sure you have your snacks handy. We'll have an intermission in about 40 minutes, so you can load up on more snacks and take a bathroom break then.

I also want you to listen for something during the movie. Every time you hear the line, "To infinity and beyond," I want you to yell back, "Buzz Lightyear to the rescue!"

Let's practice that three times.

Practice shouting the response three times, then remind kids to do it each time they hear the cue in the movie. Close the Opening Credits by saying: **Let's go on a *Toy Story* adventure...to infinity and beyond!**

Dim the lights and turn off the CD player as the movie begins. Be prepared to start the intermission about 34 minutes into the film, when Buzz and Woody are on their way to Pizza Planet in the truck and Woody gets smashed by the toolbox.

Intermission (20 minutes)

Once you've paused the movie, gradually turn the lights back on, and return to the front of the room. Ask for several volunteers to share their answers to these questions:

- **How do you think Woody felt when Buzz arrived?**
- **Why was Woody jealous?**
- **Why do you think Woody's jealousy is dangerous?**

Say: **It looks like they're in for quite an adventure! In about 15 minutes, we'll start the movie again. This is a great time to load up on snacks at our very own Pizza Planet snack table and use the bathroom.**

We're also going to play some games. Please stand up and stretch out your arms all the way to the side. These are your wings. We're going to play To Infinity and Beyond!

This first game is designed to get kids moving around after sitting for 40 minutes. Create four groups of kids (and parents, too!), and have each group move to a different corner of the room. Give each group a number. Explain that you'll call out two numbers. When kids hear their group's number, they're to fly like Buzz Lightyear and switch places with the other group you called. When you say, "To infinity and beyond," all groups will launch, flying to the opposite corner.

Call pairs of numbers for a few minutes. Make sure you say, "To infinity and beyond" several times during the game.

Say: **Each of you would make a great Buzz Lightyear! Now find a partner. Decide who is the "Slinky toy" and who is the "top." In the second half of our movie, Buzz and Woody have to work together, and I'm going to let you pairs of toys work together too.**

Give each pair a roll of toilet paper, and have the Slinky toys wrap the toilet paper around the eyes of the tops so the tops can't see.

Say: **You have to work together to get to Pizza Planet and then back to the screening area where we're watching the movie. Without touching their partners, the Slinky toys will guide the tops to Pizza Planet. Then you'll switch, and the Slinky toys will be blindfolded and guided back to the screening area.**

Facilitate kids during this activity, and when everyone is back in the screening area—and you've had kids place the shreds of paper in garbage bags—continue.

Say: **I told you earlier that this movie reminds me of two brothers who had a problem. The older brother was very jealous of the younger brother. Just as Woody tried to "terminate" Buzz, the older brother terminated the younger one. The older brother's jealousy was so dangerous that it hurt his brother. I'll tell you what happened after the movie. For now, make sure you have your snack from Pizza Planet, and let's finish the movie.**

When everyone is ready, dim the lights, and begin the movie where you paused it.

Closing Credits (12 minutes)

Say: **Turn to a partner, and tell that person what your favorite part of the movie was.**

While the moviegoers talk, quietly play the "Toy Time" track on the *More Than a Movie* CD (track 22), and turn up the lights. After about a minute of discussion, ask for volunteers to share what their favorite part was. Then ask pairs to discuss the following questions. Ask:

- **What did Woody do to become friends with Buzz?**
- **What did Buzz do to become friends with Woody?**
- **How was jealousy dangerous in this movie?**
- **What things are we sometimes jealous about?**
- **How can our jealousy become dangerous to others—and ourselves?**

Say: **My favorite part of this movie was that Buzz and Woody became good friends and helped each other. Woody was jealous of Buzz, but he got over it, and they became friends!**

We can do the same thing in our lives when we're jealous. The brothers I was telling you about earlier didn't do that. That's because the older brother was so jealous that he *killed* his younger brother. Jealousy turned into anger and rage.

When the older brother did this, God was angry with him. So through the rest of the older brother's life, he had many problems.

Jealousy can be very dangerous—for everyone.

We all feel jealousy sometimes, but let's not let jealousy become a problem for us. Instead, let's decide to let the love of God replace it in our hearts!

That's tonight's movie! You've been a great audience. Good night!

Additional Themes Illustrated by This Movie:

courage, guilt, loneliness, and sacrifice

WHERE THE RED FERN GROWS

In the Spotlight:

The Point: Some things come at a great price.

As your children watch a young boy work to buy and train a pair of hunting dogs, they'll consider how some things come at a great price—including their salvation.

The Passage: John 15:12-13

"My command is this: Love each other as I have loved you. Greater love has no one than this, that he lay down his life for his friends."

Notes to the Director

Where the Red Fern Grows has a running time of 97 minutes, so you'll have just 23 minutes to help children make the connection between the sacrifices made in the movie and the ultimate sacrifice Jesus made for their salvation.

Environment

This movie is all about dogs!

To set the mood, collect as many stuffed dogs as you can, and use them to decorate the room. For added fun, encourage children when you advertise your movie night to bring along a favorite stuffed dog. Photocopy raccoon pictures, and hide them around the room, making some easy to find and some harder to find. Make as many copies of the raccoon picture on page 97 as you'd like!

And be sure to play the "Howling Hounds" track of the *More Than a Movie* CD (track 23) as children arrive. Set your CD player on "repeat" so the track plays non-stop until the Opening Credits.

Carry the theme through to the snacks by serving pretzel rods and sticks.

Cautions

This movie contains several scenes that might frighten very young children and should be shown with *great* caution to anyone not in the upper-elementary age group. This movie contains questionable language, violence, blood, and the death of both a child and animals.

If you expect to have young children at your *More Than a Movie* event, it would be best to not show this selection. For upper elementary-age children, it raises significant issues that will prompt a good discussion.

G | GENERAL AUDIENCES
All Ages Admitted

1974, Doty-Dayton
Releasing
Running time: 97 minutes

CAUTION

Supplies

- CD player
- *More Than a Movie* CD
- pretzel rods and sticks
- disposable bowls for pretzels
- photocopies of raccoons
- two large candy bars
- one jar of baby food peas
- two plastic spoons

Opening Credits (6 minutes)

Gradually turn down the volume of the CD track. Appear wearing bib overalls and, if possible, a coonskin hat.

Say: **Welcome to our *More Than a Movie* night! We're screening *Where the Red Fern Grows*, a film about great sacrifice. One of the meanings of sacrifice is to give something up.**

Turn to someone sitting next to you, and tell that person one thing you'd be willing to give up for someone else and why. You've got 20 seconds.

Ask for several volunteers to share what they'd give up and for whom.

Say: **In this movie, we're going to see a young boy work hard to earn enough money to buy what he's always wanted: a pair of hunting dogs. He's willing to do whatever it takes to get those dogs.**

Before we screen the movie, let's see how willing you are to get something you might want. I need two volunteers. Choose two children from the audience who you think will accept the challenge!

Show the two children and the audience the candy bars.

Say: **How would you like to have one of these candy bars? Are you willing to do something to get one?** After each question, give the volunteers a chance to answer and do what you have asked them to do. If a child *won't* do the actions, give him or her a candy bar anyway.

- **Would you be willing to give me a hug?**
- **Would you be willing to touch your toes four times?**
- **Would you be willing to eat a spoonful of these peas?**

You guys were great! Thanks for playing my game. Here are your candy bars; you may take your seats.

Those were pretty harmless things they had to do to get a candy bar. In our movie, Billy is going to have to be willing to do a *lot* more to get his dogs. And later, the sacrifices he's made to get the dogs may seem like they've come at a very great price.

Do you all have your snacks? The big pretzel rods remind me of tree trunks, and the little ones remind me of tree branches! In our movie, the dogs are going to "tree" the raccoons. This means that the dogs will chase the raccoons up the trees and out onto the branches. We'll have an intermission in about an hour, and that will be the time to load up on more tree trunks and branches and take a bathroom break.

[Handwritten margin notes: "Have you ever wanted something so bad & your parents said you would have to pay for it?" and "What does sacrifice mean."]

One more thing: During this movie, you'll see a tree being chopped down. When it starts to fall, I want you to yell, "Timber!" Let's practice that on the count of three.

Lead children and adults in shouting "Timber!" then close the Opening Credits by saying: **Release the hounds!**

Dim the lights after you start the movie.

Be prepared to start the intermission about 48 minutes into the film, when you hear the line, "No coon hunter came into Grandpa's store with as many skins as I did."

Intermission (10 minutes)

Once you have paused the movie, gradually turn the lights back on, and return to the front of the room.

Say: **Wow! Can you believe how well Billy and Old Dan and Little Ann hunt? In 10 minutes we'll resume our movie, so this is a great time to take a bathroom break or get another bowl of tree trunks and branches!**

Join me in standing up, please. We're going to play a game while we take our intermission. Turn the "Howling Hounds" track from the CD (track 23) back on.

I'd like to see how well *you* hunt too. First hunt up a partner. Everyone needs someone to work with in this game.

The person in your pair with the longest fur—that's hair—will be the hunting dog; the other person will be the hunter! You'll trade places in a minute, so it doesn't matter who's in which role first!

I've hidden pictures of raccoons around the room. When I say, "Release the hounds," I want the hunting dogs to sniff and search for a raccoon. When you find one, howl loudly so your hunter can come and get the raccoon.

Every time your team finds a raccoon, trade places and start again.

Give pairs several minutes to find the raccoons, then quiet them down. Have each pair count how many raccoons they've found. Cheer for all those who went hunting, then turn off the CD player.

Encourage moviegoers to get any additional snacks they want and settle in for the rest of the movie. Dim the lights, and pick up the movie where you paused it.

Closing Credits (7 minutes)

Say: **While you're still thinking about the movie, quickly turn to a parent or partner, and discuss this question:**

• Who made the greatest sacrifice in the movie and why? You've got one minute to talk.

After a minute has passed, ask for several volunteers to share how they answered the question. Affirm their answers, then say: **There were a lot of sacrifices made in this movie. Billy sacrificed a lot of playtime to work and save enough money to buy his dogs.**

Billy sacrificed winning the competition so he could save Grandpa.

Old Dan sacrificed his life for his master and friend when he saved Billy from the mountain lion.

John 15:12-13 says, "My command is this: "Love each other as I have loved

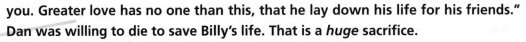

you. Greater love has no one than this, that he lay down his life for his friends."
Dan was willing to die to save Billy's life. That is a *huge* sacrifice.

And it's a sacrifice that someone has made for you.

Jesus came to earth knowing that he was going to make the ultimate sacrifice. He came to die on the cross so we could live forever with him in heaven if we believe in him.

If you don't know about Jesus and what he did for you, hang around after we finish tonight, and I'd be happy to tell you about it.

That's our movie tonight—thanks and good night!

Additional Themes Illustrated by This Movie:

determination, love, loyalty, and perseverance

Permission to photocopy this handout from *More Than a Movie* granted for local church use.
Copyright © Group Publishing, Inc., P.O. Box 481, Loveland, CO 80539. www.group.com

4 CHILDREN'S MINISTRY FILM FESTIVALS

Film festivals are fun and involving,
and they encourage your kids to serve.
Here's how to hold a festival at your church!

A film festival requires just three things:
• an audience
• a venue
• films to screen

You've got the audience: kids in your ministry and their parents.

The venue is simple: your church or any other place that has a video projector, a screen, and someplace for people to sit.

And the films? They're short projects you'll prepare with children or that children will prepare themselves with (or without) the help of parents. Collect three or more five-minute videos created by your kids, roll out the red carpet, and screen those videos all at one time—you've got yourself a film festival!

It doesn't have to be difficult, and it can be a ton of fun.

Why Host a Film Festival?

For starters, it's important to understand what a children's ministry film festival is not.

It's *not* a high-profile juried show where someone goes home with a trophy for producing the best/most original/most unusual film for children.

Rather, a children's ministry film festival is a time where short videos produced by children in your ministry are screened for the enjoyment of an audience. There's no jury of experts, and there's no trophy. The goal isn't to win a prestigious award.

Instead, your goal is to have children participate in a hands-on project that facilitates deep learning.

Creating videos and hosting a children's ministry film festival doesn't require a lot of funding. You probably have all or most of the resources needed to pull off the event (more on this later).

And when you host a film festival, you can expect a significant number of parents to show up. If a child in your ministry writes, acts in, does a voice-over for, or otherwise contributes to a film, you can bet that the child's parents will attend the premiere.

It's like the annual Christmas pageant: Even if a child lands the role of Third Sheep From the Left, a proud parent will be there with a video camera rolling.

A film festival is all about involvement—and you can build involvement if you intentionally select video projects that encourage it. Ten examples of possible video projects you can do in your ministry are on pages 101-107.

Also, film festivals allow artistic kids in your ministry to have a voice and to contribute in a unique way to the life of your church. It's not as if you're letting those visual kids redecorate the Sunday school classrooms on a regular basis. Film projects help artistic kids develop their God-given gifts and use them in a significant way.

Finally, the clincher: Creating videos and hosting a film festival doesn't require a massive number of adult volunteers…and might actually turn out to be a money-maker for your children's ministry! Someone will be providing popcorn, so sell it at a profit!

If you're reading this book, you're not afraid of using movies in your church. You already know the value of video. A film festival takes that appreciation a step further—and involves your kids as contributors rather than as a passive audience.

Stick with us, and consider whether a homegrown film festival might be a ministry opportunity that would capture your children. See if it's something God wants you to champion in your church.

But first, there's a question to answer: If you want to host a children's ministry film festival, where will you find the videos to show? You can't screen videos you haven't created.

Coming up are three ways that the production of four- and five-minute videos can become a valued and natural part of your children's ministry. Two of the approaches provide enough films to fill the handbill of a film festival.

Film Source No. 1: Service Team Moviemaking

Larry Shallenberger credits others with the notion of having a team of children create videos that feature action figures as actors, but he's found a way to make the process his own.

"Each Wednesday night, we have a service team of kids who film a script that connects with the next Sunday's children's church," Larry says. Those four- to five-minute videos might illustrate a Bible story or expand on a Bible point. Either way, says Larry, "The kids on Sunday morning love the videos."

On Wednesday night, it all starts with a script Larry has pulled from puppet books or that has been written especially for the program. Visit www.group.com to find puppet script books for sale.

Locating scripts hasn't been a huge challenge for Shallenberger, who has written some of the scripts himself. He mines his collection of puppet script books and finds it's fairly easy to adapt existing scripts.

"You could also get extremely student-centered and ask your junior highers to write scripts," says Shallenberger, though he hasn't yet taken that step.

Once a script is in hand, the Wednesday night team is divided into two groups: the actors and the readers.

The **actors** review the script and then pull out action figures to play the roles in the script.

That's right: *action figures*. Those endlessly varied, ever-popular toys so easily found at thrift shops and yard sales become the on-screen actors for each of Shallenberger's video creations.

The actors don't actually appear on screen, at least from the wrist up. They're responsible for creating quick sets and then moving the action figures around on stage. It's the *action figures* that are tightly framed by the videographer and that appear in the video.

"We don't give kids the final say on which action figures will appear on screen," Shallenberger says. "You don't want three Incredible Hulks or Spider-Mans running around in the same video. It confuses the audience on Sunday morning."

On-Screen Talent for Free!

Start your collection of action figures with an appeal for church families to empty their toy chests of unwanted action figures, Barbie and Ken dolls, and related paraphernalia. You'll be amazed at how fast your collection grows!

Once the actors have sorted out the visuals and decided which action figures represent which characters, they block the action. That is, they decide who will control which figure and how the figures will move around in front of the camera.

A quick rehearsal and they're ready to go.

The **readers** perform voice-overs that will provide the soundtrack for the video. They're capable readers who perform the script with all the emotion and enthusiasm they can muster.

Please note that not all readers are created equal. Some children are simply more skilled at reading and more expressive than others. In creating the soundtrack, you'll be forced to decide what you value most: ministry or production values.

Strike a balance between the two.

You can't create effective videos if children reading the soundtrack stumble over words. Rehearsing the lines helps, but there must be a fundamental skill match with the task at hand.

But you don't want to surrender kids' involvement in favor of using adults who have better reading voices. This is a hands-on kids project!

Once readers rehearse (and rewrite lines that are too complex or that won't play well with your audience), it's time to record.

Shallenberger reports that recording several readings of the soundtrack and shooting several takes of the visuals can be accomplished in about 45 minutes. Plan on taking longer the first few times you create a video; things go more smoothly with practice.

Of course, those 45 minutes yield just raw footage. Several hours of someone's time are required for editing each video, which leads to the final team that's required for video creation: the tech team.

Before You Go Surfing for Audio Special Effects…

Do yourself a favor and install a pop-up locker and a spyware blocker on your computer. Free sites are often used to flood your computer with marketing information.

The **tech team** shapes material created by the children into a presentable form. At Shallenberger's church, he works very closely with the tech team—because it's usually Larry himself.

"It takes me between two and three hours to edit a four- to five-minute video," says Shallenberger. "First I dump the soundtracks and video into my computer, then I start by establishing the soundtrack."

Once the soundtrack is ready, Shallenberger drops in the visuals to match the soundtrack. Because the visuals were shot as someone read the script aloud, the timing of the audio and visual elements are in synch.

Then comes the fun: Shallenberger adds elements like title pages and royalty-free sound effects he'd downloaded from the Internet. There's no shortage of free sites that provide ambient sounds such as seashores, storms, and the quick "pop, crackle, and thump" special effects that add drama and fun.

If you've ever edited videos on a computer, you quickly discover that audio and video files consume massive amounts of memory. Many computers designed for home use are quickly overwhelmed—and a computer with insufficient memory is a showstopper for a tech team.

Shallenberger added an additional hard drive to his computer to handle video editing, and he also purchased specialty software.

"The software I bought isn't a cheap date," Shallenberger admits. "I spent about $400. But the moviemaker program built into Windows XP can provide usable quality, and it's part of the package."

Again, it's a trade-off, this time between programming quality and budget. Professional quality comes at a steep price. There's a reason why commercially available live-action "kid vids" easily cost $1,500 per minute of finished video to produce.

One way to avoid paying top dollar and sweating every edit detail is to intentionally go for a "campy" look in your videos. Remember the look and feel of the original Batman episodes, when you were likely to see Adam West climbing a rope up a building? It was obvious that the camera had simply been tipped onto one side and West was really walking along a stage—but who cared? It all worked.

You're videotaping Spider-Man figures and Barbie dolls. You won't have to work all that hard to hit "campy" and have it work for you and your tech team. But you absolutely must have this equipment:

• A computer that has the capacity to handle editing

How big is big enough? That depends on the program you're using. Start by finding out what hardware is available for your use. See what video editing software is already installed, and determine if it will meet your needs. Then see if there's sufficient memory—especially RAM memory—available to let you do what you need to do quickly and efficiently.

A word to the wise: If you're not a "tech-y" sort of person, *recruit someone who is*. Without the right hardware and software, you're sunk. Be sure you're working with good information.

• A digital video camera—one with a shotgun microphone if possible

Your camera and computer editing system need to play nice and talk to each other, so be sure everything is compatible and you have the cables and cords you need.

You can survive without a good microphone attached to the camera, but it makes things easier if you can record the visual *and* audio tracks simultaneously.

And while you're shopping, begging, or borrowing, ask for a tripod, too.

• A microphone for your readers

Haven't got a good microphone on your camera? Don't worry—if you create a separate audio track, you can import the audio track on its own...maybe. Be sure your computer and software can handle this task.

And when selecting a microphone, get an *omnidirectional* one that allows several children to sit around it and talk at the same time. Some microphones have a "sweet spot" that lets only one speaker be recorded at a time and from a very specific direction. It's not useful when you're using an ensemble cast.

If you have someone who runs a soundboard at your church, this is the person to bring in for a consultation.

There are two ways to capture the audio track.

The cheapest way is to amplify the readers through a public address system and capture it with the video camera. You're assured that the audio and visuals will be in synch, but you'll get some distortion. Good movie editing software will allow you to "scrub" a lot of the distortion out.

The other approach is to record audio tracks to a recordable CD or an audio-tape, which lets you capture cleaner tracks. However, the trade-off is that you'll have to line up the audio and video tracks manually.

• Lighting

Purists will suggest that nothing less than a balanced set of spotlights will work. Those people are clearly not working with a children's ministry department budget.

Think spotlights clamped wherever they're needed to light the set area. The ones you'll find at a home-supply store will do the job. Plus, those big-box stores have every conceivable sort of light bulb, too.

Experiment, but do so on the cheap. If you have a decent camera, it will be forgiving of some of the lighting inadequacies.

• A tabletop

Since you're using action figures, a small stage is all you need. Several kids will be moving the figures around, so you'll need a stage that's easy for a group of children to gather around. All in all, a tabletop fits the bill nicely.

Use a light, solid-colored tabletop so there's high contrast between the action figures and the tabletop.

• Supplies for backdrops

If you want your action figures to walk through a city, your background can be as simple as building outlines quickly sketched on poster paper. A countryside background can be tree shapes. We're not talking about anything complicated or terribly time-consuming to create.

Remember that you can establish a background in part by downloading a sound clip that sets the stage (waves on a beach, city traffic, or wind in trees).

But a simple backdrop is still useful—and can be created by your kids.

• Scripts

Scour your church library for skit books, puppet books, and drama productions. Look around on the Internet for resources—there are dozens of sites and hundreds of sources for scripts. You'll probably have to adapt whatever you find, so try not to spend outrageous amounts of money here.

That said, *do* consider purchasing "instant skit" books where the soundtrack is already complete. These are often available at a cost of less than $2 per script, including the complete soundtrack. It's a bargain if you're tight on time during one particular week or if the program you tried to create crashed and burned.

• **Action figures**

You'll need a large box packed with them, including props that might be useful along the way.

When you're first starting, go for quantity. Take whatever people will give you and whatever good deal you find at the yard sale down the street.

After you've assembled a sizable collection, start tossing the horse figures that only have three legs and the Barbie whose hair was chopped off.

Film Source No. 2: A Class Project

Maybe setting up shop for weekly video production doesn't appeal to you. You don't have the time and interest, or there's no logical place for the videos in your children's ministry programming.

Then consider this instead: Create just *one* video as a class project.

You'll still need the same resources required for an ongoing program, but there's a key difference: You don't need regular access to those resources. That means you need to find just one person in your church who has the equipment and who enjoys creating videos, and you need to recruit that person as a one-project volunteer. Make sure that the person can work with you and your kids, and run the volunteer through the same background checks you'd do on any other volunteer.

But be clear that the commitment is to one project.

Before you suggest the project to your kids, be sure you've lined up all the resources. You'll need your volunteer and a place to screen the video when it's complete. That can be in "big people's church" or as part of a larger film festival. And be sure you've clearly defined the scope of the project:

How long should the video be? Is there a budget? When will children work on it—in class or outside of class? What's the timeline? Who will handle the script writing, the casting, and the production? Who will handle the postproduction work? Who will loan your kids the equipment needed to make the project happen?

A suggestion: Scale the projects so they can be completed in class. You'll vastly increase participation.

Here are some ideas you can develop for a film project. Each one has great possibilities to develop as a learning experience, too.

Family Faith Story

Ask children to interview their parents about their family's faith development. How does each family celebrate and encourage growth in Christian faith? What actions and attitudes support that growth? What do parents want for their children in terms of a relationship with Jesus?

Debriefing Directions: What does it mean to "raise up a child in the way he should go?" What role should faith play in a family?

A Heritage of Faith

Children will dig into the history of your congregation in this mini-documentary. If you happen to be a church that's a century old, there may be a *lot* of material to consider, so be clear about what you want to uncover.

The goal isn't to create a history lesson. Rather, it's to find out what core beliefs your church embraces. What cultural considerations or traditions set you apart from other churches in your town? What do you have in common with other churches?

Ask kids to interview a variety of church members—especially those who can talk from experience about "the old days" in your church.

Debriefing Directions: What are faith essentials in the kingdom of God, and what is tradition? How important is church unity to Jesus?

Fingerprints of Love

Ask children to consider a passage of Scripture that encourages Christians to interact with their culture. For example, Jesus points out that clothing and feeding the poor and visiting those in prison are important acts of service. Where is that happening in your town, your church, or your Sunday school? How can you become involved, and what might that mean to your kids?

Debriefing Directions: Can children do God's work? What are some biblical examples? current examples? What other directives are believers given in the Bible?

A Heart for the Nations

Most churches support at least one missionary who's sharing the good news somewhere in the world. Especially if the missionary works in a foreign culture, ask children to describe what the host culture is like and what the missionary is doing in that culture.

The soundtrack might include a conference call to the missionary, as well as other research done by your children.

Debriefing Directions: What is the purpose of missionary work? In what ways can children fulfill the "Great Commission"?

Built to Last

Use a brief video to tell the story of your children's ministry to adults in your church. A video designed to communicate what happens in children's ministry can be shown in the larger church worship service and can be used to inform, to recruit, and to celebrate what God is doing.

Be sure to start by clearly understanding how the video will be used and by securing permission to film children.

Debriefing Directions: What does Jesus say about children? What does a "child-like faith" mean? Why does it matter that Jesus loves us?

A Day in the Life

Ask children to write a script that shows how God works through people in their daily lives.

Focus on an adult, and follow him or her through a typical day. Or even better—follow an elementary child through a day at home and school.

This project presents some challenges: how to film a child in real time and then reduce the entire experience down to four or five minutes, how to handle the project using just interviews if filming at school isn't practical or permitted, and who to choose as a subject.

The good news: Your kids can figure it out!

Debriefing Directions: How *does* God use us? Does God use us if we aren't willing to be used? What does God want us to accomplish in daily life?

Good Advice

In this documentary, have your kids talk with older Christians in your church and ask what advice the elderly people might have for children. Be sure to explore *why* a particular piece of advice is given: Does Marie suggest obeying your parents because something happened in her life to underscore the importance of that?

Debriefing Directions: Discuss where we can go for good advice and how to recognize good advice when we hear it. In what ways is the Bible a source of good advice?

Firm Foundations

This suggestion requires at least your camera operator to work outside of class, unless you happen to meet in an area where there's residential construction underway.

Have kids visit a house that's under construction (with permission, of course!) and see how foundations are laid for houses. Then have children read Jesus' parable about building on sand and rock and draw comparisons between what they see and what they read.

Debriefing Directions: What does a house built on the rock look like in terms of the Christian life? What things are storms that threaten us? Where are we building our lives?

Commercials

Ask kids to create 30- and 60-second commercials for becoming a Christian. Encourage kids to include any benefits they think are important. You could also have kids create commercials for your church or your class.

But be aware that you're inviting kids to share what they really think. Be affirming of whatever that might be, and be grateful that you have insight into their true thinking.

Debriefing Directions: Why don't we ever talk about the costs of becoming a Christ-follower? What are those costs? What did Jesus tell his followers they could expect from their lives?

Film Source No. 3: Invite Submissions for a Film Festival

Maybe a class project isn't practical for some reason, but you still want to gather enough videos for a film festival.

Fine. Do this: Write to families and invite their participation as guest artists.

Select a theme, and outline the parameters of the project in detail. Make sure you note the *length* of submissions—both a minimum and a maximum. Be specific about how and when the film festival will be held. (Allow at least two months for videos to be received.)

Your goal is to make creating a film a *family* event, so send the invitations to children's homes addressed "to the parent of…" Ask parents to talk with their children about participating and tackling the project as a family.

If parents are interested but lack the resources, think twice about offering to put a video camera into every open hand. You probably don't have enough contacts to do that, and you won't want to find yourself responsible if something happens to the equipment.

Instead, include a paragraph that communicates that while every family may not have the video equipment needed, they certainly know someone who does. Encourage parents to arrange for their own loans of resources—loans that don't go through you.

And don't worry if you get very few submissions. You can show a "short" film or two as part of a program that features one of the full-length movie programs in this book!

Now You Have the Films...What About the Film Festival?

Have you ever watched the Academy Awards or another entertainment awards program on television? There's a red carpet…flashing cameras…adoring fans.

That's the sort of event you want—not a dry, academic evaluation of the merits of each video submission.

Each submission is a winner because it reflects both initiative and involvement. And—if you were careful to see that it happened—the experience of creating the video has translated into debriefing and application. There's been learning.

The only thing left is to celebrate the creativity that's been expressed!

Even if you have to bribe the youth group with pizzas, have a small crowd with flash attachments on their cameras waiting to welcome the moviemakers to their grand premiere. Rope off a fan section where teenagers can ask for autographs, and have a red carpet outside the door to the screening room. Do it up right!

Introduce the people responsible for each video, and leave room for questions after each one. If you've had the submissions address a single theme, you'll have the chance to explore an issue in-depth.

Whatever else you ask, dive deep into applying what has been learned and identifying specific follow-up actions children (and adults) can take.

After the screenings, announce that there will be a gala celebration, and wheel in the snacks as you crank up the party music. It's party time!

Your film festival can be as complex or as simple as you wish. It can be low-budget or a significant expense. It can be a one-time event or an annual tradition.

However you tailor your film festival, be sure that it's an opportunity for children to deepen their faith in Jesus.

THEMES INDEX

Use the movies selected for this book to illustrate these topics:

SCRIPTURE INDEX

EVALUATION FOR
More Than a Movie

Please help Group Publishing, Inc., continue to provide innovative and useful resources for ministry. Please take a moment to fill out this evaluation and mail or fax it to us. Thanks!

Group Publishing, Inc.
Attention: Product Development
P.O. Box 481
Loveland, CO 80539
Fax: (970) 292-4370

● ● ●

1. As a whole, this book has been (circle one)
   not very helpful   *very helpful*
   1   2   3   4   5   6   7   8   9   10

2. The best things about this book:

3. Ways this book could be improved:

4. Things I will change because of this book:

5. Other books I'd like to see Group publish in the future:

6. Would you be interested in field-testing future Group products and giving us your feedback? If so, please fill in the information below:

Name_____

Church Name _____

Denomination _____   Church Size _____

Church Address _____

City _____   State _____   ZIP _____

Church Phone_____

E-mail _____

Permission to photocopy this page granted for local church use.
Copyright © Group Publishing, Inc., P.O. Box 481, Loveland, CO 80539. www.group.com

BibleVenture
centers™

Group

BibleVenture centers™
Jesus—Death Destroyer

4 weeks with Jesus

BibleVenture centers™
Moses—Powered by God

4 weeks with Moses

Reproducibles Included

BibleVenture centers™
Paul—Shackled & Shipwrecked

4 weeks with Paul

CD & Reproducibles Included

Four **COMPLETE, READY-TO-GO**
lessons help children's ministry
leaders **ENGAGE MULTIPLE**
LEARNING STYLES with
memorable Bible learning. **CD**
and **REPRODUCIBLES INCLUDED.**

Order today at **www.group.com**
or call **1-800-747-6060 ext.1370**

CD & Reproducibles Included